LIVING THE WISDOM OF ST. FRANCIS

Living the Wisdom
of St. Francis

Wayne Simsic

 PAULIST PRESS ● New York/Mahwah, N.J.

All psalms are taken from Nancy Schreck, O.S.F., and Maureen Leech, O.S.F., *Psalms Anew* (Winona, Minn.: St. Mary's Press, 1986). All other scripture quotes are from the *New Revised Standard Version* (New York: Oxford University Press, 1989).

Cover and interior illustration by John B. Giuliani, The Benedictine Grange, West Redding, CT 06896

Cover design by Cheryl Finbow

Library of Congress Cataloging-in-Publication Data

Simsic, Wayne,
Living the wisdom of St. Francis / Wayne Simsic.
p. cm.
Includes bibliographical references.
ISBN 0-8091-4050-0 (alk. paper)
1. Francis, of Assisi, Saint, 1182–1226—Meditations. 2. Catholic Church—Prayer-
books and devotions—English. 3. Spiritual life—Catholic Church. I. Title: Living
the wisdom of Saint Francis. II. Title.
BX4700.F6 S535 2001
271'.302—dc21
2001036326

Published by
Paulist Press
997 Macarthur Boulevard
Mahwah, New Jersey 07430

www.paulistpress.com

Printed and bound in the United States of America

TABLE OF CONTENTS

This book
is dedicated
to the memory of
Laura Urgo,
who gave her heart
so generously to the poor.

Acknowledgments

I would like to thank all those, too numerous to list, who have shared with me their passion for the Franciscan spirit. They have left their mark on this book as surely as if they had a hand in the actual writing of it. I am especially grateful to participants in my retreats who have opened up their hearts to me.

A sincere thank you to those who have had a part in the shaping of this work, particularly Donna Crilly, my editor.

Most importantly, I thank my wife, Diana, for her loving support and guidance while this book unfolded and for encouraging my enthusiasm for Francis from the beginning.

INTRODUCTION

I cried aloud to God,
with praise on my tongue.
    —Psalm 66:17

One evening, I followed a trail that led to
the crumbling Rocco fortress on the hilltop just above the
town of Assisi. As the sun began its journey toward the horizon, I found a clear view of the valley below and watched
waves of light recede, leaving deepening shadows and
splashes of purple and rose pastels in their wake.

Behind me, a group began to chant psalms, and I imagined
Francis and a band of friars, singing and dancing their way
through this mysterious and beautiful Umbrian landscape,
praising the Creator in harmony with the rhythm of light
and the deeper music of all creation. I was captivated by the
image of Francis immersed in the landscape from morning to
evening. He walked through fields in the coolness of early
morning, his eyes dancing with the heads of flowers and
long-stemmed grain that swayed in a breeze, his heart welcoming the rising sun. In the afternoon heat, the scent of dry,
hot grass mingled with the smell of sweat; in the cool of early
evening, he offered thanks and shared a simple meal of

bread, fruit, and water with his brothers. He rested under thickets, in caves, or under the blanketing stars.

Francis gestured, danced, laughed, and sang; felt the earth in his skin and bones; talked with Jesus; enjoyed the companionship of his brothers; and preached repentance in towns along the way. From the time of his conversion, he envisioned himself as the troubadour of Christ. On occasion, he would pick up a stick and, imagining that he was playing a violin, sing about his God. He refused to suppress the energy of his soul and coaxed his brothers to sing so that they would awaken the spirit of joy in the hearts of listeners.

Francis's life itself became a song because he was open to the Spirit working through him. All that he did was a response to the creative dynamism of the Spirit that gave him the strength to reach out in an affectionate and immediate way to his brothers; to the poor, the sick, and all those pushed to the margins of society; to all creation, including creatures small or forgotten. Because he opened his heart so completely, the song flowed through him and became a way of living, an ongoing prayer of gratitude and praise.

The short meditations that compose this book introduce the joyful, singing saint in a way that invites participation. Today, perhaps more than ever before, we are looking for a song that heals the separation we experience with ourselves, with others, with Earth and cosmos, and with God. Francis's own song found its rhythm in Christ, both the historical Christ who lived and died for us and the Word made flesh who can be found in our hearts and at the center of all creation. Through Christ, he guides us home.

You are invited to uncover the song of the Spirit in your own life with Francis as your guide. Though he lived eight hundred years ago, the little poor man of Assisi speaks clearly to our hearts today. He offers us a new consciousness, a new practice, and a new vision. Those who walk with him, even for a short time, often hear a chord struck in the depths of their heart, one they will not easily forget. "I think Francis of Assisi is in the depths of every human being, for all are touched by grace," writes Carlo Carretto. Many would agree.

I
Toward a Sense of Kinship

The Franciscan universe is never dead...
Everything makes up a grand symphony—
and God is the conductor.
—Leonardo Boff,
Cry of the Earth, Cry of the Poor

These first meditations introduce fundamental steps toward joining Francis in song. They include primary Franciscan themes such as conversion; God's abundant goodness and love; humility, poverty, and simplicity; and our membership, humanity and creation alike, in a divine family.

By focusing attention on our relatedness to all beings, Francis calls us beyond ourselves to let go of barriers and fears and become kin with all creation. He asks us to sing praise to the Creator in unison with a community that includes the poor, outcasts, and all other beings. Such singing teaches us to live wisely in our shared planetary home.

LIVING GOSPEL VALUES

The rule and life of the friar minor is this:...to follow the teaching and the footprints of our Lord Jesus Christ.

—The Earlier Rule

We may realize the importance of the gospel message and even reflect on it, but do we bother to live it? Francis realized that if there was to be an authentic change in his life, he needed to live gospel values. He took his cue from passages that outlined a call to discipleship and identification with the poor.

During his solitude in a cave on Mount Subasio, Francis reviewed his life and became overwhelmed by the sheer weight of his brokenness. He wept. The truth transformed his heart, and in the darkness, a light appeared and grew stronger. It instilled in him a deep desire to follow the gospel message. He wished to listen carefully to the Word and, as a disciple of Jesus, to make his home in the Word and dwell in it. His calling could be summarized in a passage from John 14:23: "If anyone loves me, he will keep my word; and my Father will love him, and we will come to him, and we will make our home in him."

Because Jesus freely chose to bring good news to the poor and showed a special love for them, Francis wanted to imitate

3

Christ and work with social outcasts and the poor, something he had never imagined himself doing. He had always possessed a generous spirit but struggled to identify with those in need. In fact, he admits in his final testament that the turning point in his conversion was his willingness to serve lepers. The change came when he left behind the security of his social structure and comfortable lifestyle to care for the lepers and the poor, to spend time with them and eat with them. Living with the poor awakened him to the poverty of those in need and to the poverty and suffering of Christ.

Francis's response to living the gospel challenges the typical social categories that define our lives and keep us isolated from each other. By living among the poor lepers and the sick, and by welcoming everyone whether friend or enemy, he prods us toward a wider understanding of community, one in which no one is excluded. He reminds us that God can be found in the poor, sick, lonely, unemployed, and powerless because God is known in vulnerability. This image of a vulnerable, poor God is at the heart of Francis's spirituality. This is what encouraged him to seek out the weakest members of his society.

With Francis's example in mind, we need first to take the poor, the sick, and the oppressed to heart, knowing that God has a special love for them and that it is impossible to love God if we shun our brothers and sisters. Love will deepen our identification with them and will eventually lead to action on their behalf. This is a risk because, like Francis, our vision of life will change when we live the gospel message. Our solidarity with those in need will mean seeing the world through their eyes. We will no longer see ourselves limited to a particular socioeconomic class. We will begin to hear the "cry of the poor" in all human beings.

Echoing the spirit of Francis, Dorothy Day suggests, "We must love to the point of folly, and we are indeed fools, as Our Lord Himself was...."

Take time to be with those who are impoverished in body or spirit. Discover first hand how easy it is to be comfortable in our isolation and to be satisfied with a limited vision of the human community.

Prayer

Merciful God...by your grace alone, may we make our way to You.

—St. Francis

BECOMING GOD'S FOOL

...Now I can say without reservation, Our Father who art in heaven [Matt 6:9], since I have placed all my treasures and hope in him.
—St. Bonaventure, *The Life of St. Francis*

We tend to fill our lives with responsibilities to jobs, family, and community. There is little spare time. We stay occupied, and unscheduled time makes us nervous. What would happen if we realized that Christ was whispering to us in the midst of our life experiences—our friendships, work, and pleasures—and expected a response? Would we answer by trying to fit faith into our schedule, or would we make harder choices?

When Francis first heard the inner call, he sensed that he was no longer the same person; he could no longer live in the old way. His response was to retreat to the forests and caves around Assisi so that he could pray and discover God's will. He began to place alms in the hands of beggars and to wear simple clothes. He rebuilt the razed church of San Damiano and, gazing at the crucifix one day, fell to his knees and had a sudden revelation into the heart of the suffering Jesus. Francis was certainly tempted many times to return to his old life with its security and acceptable bourgeois conventions. But an

inner voice encouraged him and gave him strength to choose
the way of love, even though it seemed harsh and bitter.
People wondered at the change in this popular young
man. Francis's father reacted strongly. When Pietro Bernar-
done discovered that Francis had taken money without per-
mission to rebuild a church, he stormed after his son and
drove him into seclusion. Eventually, in the public square at
the center of town, Francis faced his parents and the bishop
of Assisi. A crowd of curious townspeople assembled and
watched the drama unfold. Francis stripped off his clothes as
a sign that he relinquished his past and would dedicate his
life to the spirit of poverty. He also proclaimed that he would
no longer be bound to an earthly father but only to his God
in heaven. Francis chose a path of nakedness, of birth into a
new and abundant life. He had chosen to be God's fool,
believing that those who lose their lives will save them.
His father looked on in disbelief, and the townspeople
responded with shock and sadness.

Francis left Assisi singing. His heart was free and filled
with joy. Even robbers who ripped the cloak off his back and
threw him into a snowy culvert could not diminish his
enthusiasm. He had begun a new life, and jubilation poured
out of his heart.

Francis's conversion seems dramatic to us today. But his
response to the call of faith reminds us that the way of Jesus
is foolish. It subverts our previous vision of life and causes
upheaval. It certainly demands more than a change in schedule. We have to let go of our traditional bonds, old securities,
certainties, our inherited cultural mindset and forge a new
way of life. This happens gradually over time and with the
help of grace, but soon we will find ourselves embarking on a

radically new way of life. We will wake up one day and realize that our lives were never meant to be ours but to be handed over to the deepest love we know.

How have you made room for God in your life today?

Prayer

> Let us desire nothing else
> let us wish nothing else
> let nothing else please us
> and cause us delight
> except our Creator and Redeemer and Savior,
> the one true God,
> Who is the Fullness of Good.
>
> —St. Francis

A PASSION FOR BEAUTY

The beauty of the fields, the pleasantness of the vineyards, and whatever else was beautiful to look upon could stir in him no delight. He wondered at the sudden change that had come over him.
—Thomas of Celano, *First Life of St. Francis*, II

For many, a serious commitment to the spiritual path means losing our capacity to enjoy the world fully. For Francis, however, conversion did not diminish his passion for the world and for people but heightened it.

Initially, Francis looked out at the Umbrian landscape, a landscape he had loved deeply since his early youth, and he felt nothing. Instead, urgency arose in his heart. Old loves had deserted him, and he sensed a growing desire to amend his life. Even the beauty of creation only reminded him that he should seek Beauty herself.

He responded by leaving behind a life of financial security, parties, popularity, and personal dreams and began to follow a path of faith. Did he lose his passion for life and for friendship? Because his heart was cleansed of self-interest, freed of possessiveness, and opened to God's love above everything else, relationships with creation and people did not diminish but became even more dynamic and fulfilling. He revered the mysterious light pervading the Umbrian landscape, and he witnessed Christ in the faces of the poor and lepers. He saw Mystery everywhere and reached out to embrace brothers, sisters, Clare, sun, rain, and larks as radiant images of Divine Presence.

Do we have access to the same passion and beauty in our own process of turning to God? Thomas Merton assures us: "We are living in a world that is absolutely transparent, and God shining through it all the time...If we abandon ourselves to God and forget ourselves, we see it sometimes, and we see it maybe frequently. God shows Himself everywhere, in everything—in people and in things and in nature and in events."

Until we turn our lives over to God, though, beauty can be deceptive. It draws us toward God but, at the same time, leaves us feeling empty and estranged. Following Francis, we return first to the Source and discover a world that is holy in itself, drenched in God's presence.

Has my passion for beauty increased over the years or has it lessened?

Prayer

Too late I have loved you, O Beauty of ancient days, yet ever new! Too late I have loved you! And behold, you were within, and I abroad....

—St. Augustine, *Confessions*

DIVINE ABUNDANCE

He had a crib prepared, hay carried in and an ox and an ass led to the place. The friars are summoned, the people come, the forest resounds with their voices and that venerable night is rendered brilliant and solemn by a multitude of bright lights and by resonant and harmonious hymns of praise.

—St. Bonaventure, *The Life of St. Francis*

One of the most beautiful and powerful events related in Franciscan literature is Francis's recreation of the Christmas tableau in the little hill town of Greccio.

Imagine that you are one of the pilgrims on that Christmas Eve in 1223. You begin your journey just before midnight at the foot of the mountain. With candle in hand, you and your companions slowly climb a winding path to the prepared cave. Voices and singing fill the night, and you can see a necklace of candlelight wrap around the mountain almost transforming night into day.

You arrive at the cave where a little man with dark features, dressed in a tattered cloak, presides over the celebration. Smell the fresh hay, listen to the sounds of the animals shuffling and snorting. Let your gaze rest on the small crib that holds a wooden carving of a child. Francis picks up the figure, and it seems to come alive. You embrace the child in the depths of your heart and remain silent. Mass is celebrated by a priest, and Francis, acting as a deacon, preaches on the vulnerability of a child born in an insignificant, out-of-the-way town, a child who is the fullest expression of God's love. At the conclusion of the liturgy, you depart with joyful pilgrims who sing and share their awareness of the spirit of Christ who has once again come alive in their hearts.

Fundamental to Francis's vision was the image of God entering history as a small, vulnerable child out of love for us. Francis was awestruck by the overflowing love exemplified in the incarnation. "Though he was rich beyond all things," Francis writes in a letter addressing the Christian community, "...he chose poverty." Francis discovered this love not only in the depths of humanity, but he believed that the Word of God intimately touched every particle of creation. When the Word became flesh, all physical reality received a new dignity: It became sacramental. Each creature possessed divinity and mediated divinity.

Francis found special joy not only in the humility of an infinite God who entered time but also in a God whose overwhelming love expressed itself in the eucharistic presence of Jesus. The bread is Jesus' body. It is life poured into life so that we can become strong.

What, then, is the starting point of faith for Francis? A God who became poor out of love for us. Through the example of a humble Christ, alive in the depths of our hearts and in the depths of creation, we learn the poverty and humility necessary to love others and creation as authentically as we are able. The humanity of Jesus Christ is the beginning of a new creation.

Take a moment to close your eyes and embrace the Spirit of Christ alive within you.

Prayer

We thank You
for as through Your Son You created us
so also, through Your holy love, with which You loved us
You brought about His birth.

—St. Francis

FOLLOWING CHRIST: THE CROSS

The rule and life of these brothers is this: to live in obedience, in chastity, and without anything of their own, and to follow the teaching and the footprints of our Lord Jesus Christ.

—*The Earlier Rule*

Often we question what it means to follow Christ in our lives, to live the life of the gospel.

For Francis, the call to discipleship is simple: It entails the willingness to leave all to follow Christ along the road to Calvary and beyond death to eternal life. He maps out this vision for himself and his small band of followers in his earliest rule. It includes embracing the Franciscan virtues of poverty, humility, obedience, and penitence as a means of taking the path that Christ walked.

In the end, though, the way of Jesus was primarily the way of the cross. From the early days of Francis's conversion, when he stood in front of the Byzantine cross in the razed church of San Damiano and heard Christ speaking to him, the Passion of Christ captured the saint's heart. Thomas of Celano tells us, "From then on compassion for the crucified was rooted in his holy soul...."

All the early accounts of Francis's life concentrate on his imitation of the suffering Christ. For example: He wept when he remembered Christ's Passion during prayer; his rough tunic was designed in the image of the cross; he mortified his body for the sake of Christ; and he served lepers, whom he saw as the image of the suffering Lord. He did all this because he wanted to share as perfectly as he could the experience of his beloved. He longed to be totally transformed into Christ through love.

His conformity to the Passion of Christ became complete in 1224 on Mount La Verna, when his body was marked by the wounds of Christ. From the perspective of the saint's early biographers, these wounds are best understood in the context of Francis's entire life and not as an isolated miracle. They are an external sign of a cross that had already been etched on Francis's heart through a life dedicated to imitating Christ's suffering.

This dedication to the suffering Christ is contrary to our sensibilities today; it seems unhealthy and distasteful. We think of it as a medieval devotion that is unsuitable for our lives. Yet, Francis never limited the meaning of the cross to suffering. The cross represented a vision of a world redeemed; in other words, we enter into Christ's suffering so that we can realize the power of the resurrection, particularly in a wounded world through which Christ still suffers.

The true response to this vision is not sadness but joy. Francis himself was a joyful saint who sang the praises of God and drew his brothers and all creation into a hymn of a new creation. He rebuked brothers who walked around with sad faces and counseled them to be cheerful and gracious. After receiving the stigmata, he did not retreat into dark contemplation but composed his ode to joy, the beautiful "Canticle of Brother Sun." In the end, Francis believed that it was only through the cross, through uniting with Christ in his death, that we enter into the kingdom of God and join in a "new song" of praise and thanksgiving.

How would your life be different if Christ had not sacrificed his life out of love for you?

Prayer

I want to know Christ and the power of his resurrection and the sharing of his sufferings by becoming like him in his death....

—Phil 3:10–11

KNOW THAT
YOU ARE LOVED

...He was always occupied with Jesus: Jesus he bore in his heart, Jesus in his mouth, Jesus in his ears, Jesus in his eyes, Jesus in his hands...Indeed, many times, as he went along the way meditating on and singing of Jesus, he would forget his journey and invite all the elements to praise Jesus.

—Thomas of Celano, *First Life of St. Francis, IX*

Have you ever noticed the ways in which we remember the people we love? We carry photos, place pictures in our offices, replay certain songs, bring the person's name up in conversation, and celebrate special anniversaries.

The same could be said of Francis. Wherever he went and whatever he did, Francis wanted to remember Jesus' personal love for him. One day while walking along a path, he noticed two twigs crossed, and as he stopped to reflect on Christ's sacrifice of love, tears welled up in his eyes.

It would be easy to assume that Francis recalled the suffering Christ out of guilt for past sins, but this would be a narrow interpretation. Francis had discovered the infinite possibilities of love and wanted to remain awake to the Spirit of Christ that flowed through his being and through the world. For Francis all things begin and end in Christ. He saw light shine from human faces and embraced a sacramental universe. He never felt alone because he trusted that Jesus walked at his side and was a source of divine guidance within. Is it any wonder that he sang praise with his companions and called all nature to praise Jesus? His participation in the infinite stream of love made him a mouthpiece for divine energy throughout the world.

In *The Way of the Pilgrim*, a classic text of Russian spirituality, we find how vision is transformed by remembering Jesus. A pilgrim practiced repeating the name of Jesus throughout the day for years. As the repetition took root in his unconscious, he discovered that his heart was filled with happiness and peace and his relationship with the natural world took on a sacramental quality: "Not only did I feel this in my own soul, but the whole outside world also seemed to me full of charm and delight. Everything drew me to love and thank God: people, trees, plants, and animals. I saw them all as my kinsfolk; I found on all of them the magic of the name of Jesus."

Relax, breathe deeply, and as you inhale silently, invoke the name Jesus. Practice this prayer throughout the day.

Prayer

Let all of us
wherever we are
in every place
at every hour
at every time of day

everyday and continually
believe truly and humbly
and keep in our heart
...the most high and supreme eternal God.
　　　　　　　　　—St. Francis

WITH OPEN HANDS

No one desired gold as much as he desired poverty, and no one was so careful in guarding this treasure as he was careful in guarding this pearl of the Gospel.
　　　　　　　　　　—Thomas of Celano, *Second Life of St. Francis*, XXV

When we pray, we should occasionally cup our hands and hold them open before God. This gesture represents the openness of a heart ready to trust and be filled by God's loving presence. Identifying with the humble and poor Jesus, Francis opened his own hands and heart. He became a beggar, like the ones he saw along the wayside, and trusted completely in divine providence.

One day during Mass, Francis heard the reading from Matthew in which Christ tells the disciples to go on the road and preach the gospel without money in their belts, without shoes, sandals, and staff. Francis shouted with enthusiasm, "This is what I desire with all my heart," and he proceeded to follow Christ's instructions to the letter. The words of the gospel struck his heart with full force because he realized that Christ himself embraced poverty, emptying himself for the sake of love. Should not he, Francis, follow the same path and espouse this path for others?

Francis's appreciation and understanding of poverty took time, just as it would for anyone. He embarked on a spiritual journey at the prompting of a voice of love within. Describing Francis's growth, Dorothy Day observes, "It was only later that he came to love Lady Poverty. He took it little by little; it [poverty] seemed to grow on him." First, he had to overcome his fear of lepers and then let go of his comfortable, secure life. But this process only awakened him to his deeper attachment to personal dreams of success, prestige, and power. In time, he explored the secret corners of his heart and realized that he must also confront tendencies toward pride, anger, and other habits that were preventing his inner growth.

By progressively releasing himself from attachments, Francis discovered the freedom to trust God with his whole being. His open hands, symbolic of his uncluttered heart, extended themselves toward the God on whom he truly depended for his existence and his happiness. He could no longer imagine giving wealth or any created thing an absolute value; only God was absolute. Lady Poverty, as he lovingly referred to her, had taught him a way to overcome worries and anxiety and had given him the strength to surrender his life into God's care. More importantly, Lady Poverty had revealed to him the bond he had with all human beings and with all creatures. Do we not all share our dependence on God? Are we not all called to praise the Creator?

What makes you most anxious? Practice handing it over to God again and again until its grip over you lessens. Remember that growth is measured in many small steps.

Prayer

O blessed poverty,
who bestows eternal riches on those who love and
embrace her!
O holy poverty,
to those who possess and desire you
God promises the kingdom of heaven.

—St. Clare

THE HEART'S TRUE POSTURE

Truly this is humility which exalts those who possess it, while it shows reverence to all and deserves honor from all.
　　　　　　　　—St. Bonaventure, *The Life of St. Francis*

Medieval pilgrims who visited the Basilica of St. Francis took time to "read" the images of the saint's life that were painted on the walls. They took the images to heart and used them as mirrors to reflect on their own life journey. One image they encountered while leaving the basilica was that of Francis bending over and preaching to the birds in the fields of Bevagna. It is a captivating portrait of love and tenderness that reminded the pilgrim of Francis's humble and reverent stance toward all life in imitation of Christ who was "meek and humble of heart" (Matt 11:29).

Humility today often refers to unnecessary self-negation, a posture forced on us by others or by uncomfortable circumstances. We rightfully emphasize self-worth, not the belittling of self. Yet Francis believed he was truly loved by God. Poverty had given him a true sense of self, others, and all creation as completely dependent on God.

His humble stance toward people and all creation, then, was not due to diminished self-worth or the loss of identity, but was a response to the goodness he received from the Creator and the reverence due all beings. What could he do but bow? His bow was not forced but represented his openness to God's activity in every dimension of his life. At the same time it was his response, a "yes" he said with his entire being. He allowed his whole self to be engaged by the holiness he witnessed in the world around him. In bowing, he did not lose his dignity but gained it because he acknowledged the Source of all life. Bowing was his heart's true posture, an expression of his deepest sense of self.

Francis reminds to let go of our arrogant stance in which we see ourselves standing over others and over the natural world. How can we appreciate goodness and demonstrate reverence when we exaggerate our importance? Humility calls us back to our true place in the universe as part of a web of life that sustains humanity and all creation. It is a cosmic stance because it is grounded in the Source of all life and because it responds joyfully and freely to all beings. Uncovering this humble posture of heart, we begin to heal the wounds that tear relationships apart. Humility, says Leonardo Boff in Cry of the Earth, Cry of the Poor, "is not one virtue among others, but an attitude by which we stand on the ground alongside things. From this position we can be reconciled with all things and begin a truly cosmic democracy."

How do we regain a proper sense of self in relation to others and the natural world? Following Francis, we turn to Christ for both strength and example. Although the ego tends to cultivate self-importance and control, the Spirit of Christ in us expresses itself by reaching out to others and creation. Francis would question how we can be concerned so much about ourselves when God demonstrated such humility.

Recall an experience in which you felt that God was speaking or working through you. Was this not an expression of your heart's deepest posture?

Prayer

Let us refer all good
to the Lord, God Almighty and Most High,
acknowledge that every good is His,
and thank Him....

—St. Francis

A LOVE OF SIMPLICITY

He attended always to holy simplicity....
—Thomas of Celano,
First Life of St. Francis, XVI

Francis was well known for his simple lifestyle. He refused ownership of property, preferred houses without excessive decoration, begged for food, and lived as a pilgrim in answer to the gospel command, "Be not solicitous of what you shall eat or what you shall wear....Does not your heavenly Father know you have need of these things?" (Matt 6:25—33). Like the Celtic *peregrini* (pilgrims) before him, Francis had a deep appreciation for the rhythm of the seasons, an intimacy with sun, stone, air, and sky; a preference for huts, caves, and the open sky.

The multitude of books published recently on the simple lifestyle speaks to a growing hunger for spiritual rootedness in our culture. We have lost the awareness of what is essential. We are constantly distracted by a consumerist culture that vies for our attention, pulling us in every direction with offers of a better lifestyle, the importance of doing more, and the hope of finding happiness through material things. Consumerism could be called a pseudoreligious system—its virtues are competitiveness and acquisitiveness. The result is that our desires take precedence over such values as tenderness, compassion, and community. We forget who we really are and believe that living means having.

Francis recognized that it was easy to confuse the necessities of life with the luxuries. He immediately confronted his brothers whenever they forgot the distinction. We can identify with Francis's sensitivity when we realize how quickly we identify a product as a necessity simply because it offers speed and convenience. It is difficult to part with these products because, in our desire for them, we translate them as ends rather than means. Consumption uncovers the emptiness within, an emptiness filled only by the infinite love of God.

Following Francis, we choose a simple lifestyle, not because we want to free up some time or even find peace and quiet, but because we desire to put God first. Francis followed the simple and poor life of Jesus on earth. To this end, he took the good news literally and integrated it into his life. From the time of his conversion, he saw himself as a child of God who concentrated on living the gospel life with Jesus as his model. Following this path, he became more innocent, receptive, sincere, and childlike.

This way of life is difficult for many of us to imagine. We are used to practicing time management, freeing up our schedules so that we can meet a personal goal, but do we think seriously of arranging our lives so that we can give priority to an ultimate concern? Do we appreciate that simplifying our lives in this way can affect the rest of the world?

Embracing Francis's path of simplicity, we gain the freedom to be ourselves, the desire to concentrate on what is most important for our soul, and a sense of being at home with others and the natural world. The more simple our lives become, the more room there will be in our heart to embrace the deepest peace and harmony with all.

What things or concerns have taken the place of God for you and kept you from being single hearted?

Prayer

Gracious God, my heart is bound by so many things. Give me the gift of simplicity so that I can concentrate on you above all else.

GRATEFUL FOR SMALL GIFTS

After begging one day, Francis and Brother Masseo met outside the village and found a spring and a flat stone on which to place their pieces of dried bread. Several times Francis declared to Brother Masseo that they did not deserve a treasure such as this.

Unable to understand Francis's intention, Brother Masseo responded in frustration: "Dear Father, how can this be called a treasure when there is such poverty and such a lack of things that are necessary? For here we have no cloth, no knife, no dish, no bowl, no house, no table, no waiter, no waitress."

Francis answered: "That is what I consider a great treasure— where nothing has been prepared by human labor. But everything here has been supplied by Divine Providence, as is evident in the begged bread, the fine stone table, and the clear spring...."

—The Little Flowers of St. Francis

Masseo's frustration might remind us of our own expectations not only for a good meal but for a good life—money, security, and success. We easily accept the illusion that more is better and that our happiness is linked to physical comfort. As a result, we barter away a fundamental sense of gratitude.

Francis, though, calls us back to our dependency on the Giver. Poverty and humility taught him to trust more in the providence of God and less in his own desires. As a result, he was not anxious about things he did not have and accepted whatever was given with gratitude, especially those small gifts that were unearned and unexpected. We often discover an appreciation of the simple gifts of life when we become ill or experience the death of a loved one and recognize how much we took for granted. At times like these, the world is indeed finite and insecure, and we seek out the Source of life. Small pleasures such as enjoying simple food, playing with children, holding hands with a loved one, watching a sunset, or rejoicing in beauty become immensely important. We respond by saying "thank you" with our entire being. In giving thanks, we let go of our isolation and unite ourselves to the Giver. "One who says 'Thank you' to another," explains David Steindl-Rast, "really says, 'We belong together.'"

Francis encourages us to live out of an ongoing awareness of our thankfulness. Gratitude was not an occasional acknowledgment for him but a practice of daily thanksgiving. When we acknowledge the Source of our existence through daily thanksgiving, there is less desire to consume and possess and more willingness to share. Knowing that all things are freely given, we release our selfish grip and let good things pass through us into the lives of others. Through gratitude, we experience the life of the Spirit weaving through a community, and we deepen our own sense of belonging.

Recall some of the small gifts you received today. Focus on each in turn and take a moment to give thanks.

Prayer

For all these mysteries—
For the wonder of myself,
for the wonder of your works—
I thank you.

—Psalm 139:14

A DIVINE FAMILY

When he considered the primordial source of all things, he was filled with even more abundant piety, calling creatures, no matter how small, by the name of brother or sister, because he knew they had the same source as himself.

— St. Bonaventure, *The Life of St. Francis*

The image of family has suffered in our contemporary culture. Divorce, increased mobility, consumer mentality, hectic lifestyles, and numerous other influences put pressure on the family unit. As a result, it is understandable that we might have difficulty accepting without reserve Francis's sense of a divine family.

Francis, though, leads us past any distance we might feel between the world and ourselves by focusing on the sacred Source shared by all creation. If we all share the same Parent, then certainly we are related in kinship, not only to humanity but to all creatures. The stronger our relationship with our common Parent, the greater our awareness of kinship.

Francis shatters the illusion of separateness through his love for the Creator. We are linked to all humanity, as well as to the moon, stars, forest, and streams. God is the God of people, earth, sea, sky, and all life. This awareness of a compassionate, nourishing Source of all reality moved him deeply, giving him an indescribable joy. Because of his strong sense of kinship, he became involved in a spontaneous and emotionally charged relationship with both people and creatures because he saw in all a mark of divinity. Even the smallest and most insignificant being—stone, earthworm, fields, and trees—possessed the mark of divinity and were related as brother and sister. This sensitivity to family gave him an ethical vision similar to that of Albert Schweitzer, and to the Navajo who believed that a person who behaves poorly acts without a sense of family. How can one treat a member of the family rudely without affecting others?

Family relationships are difficult. If we struggle to appreciate the divine in family members under the same roof, how can we be expected to honor our kinship with strangers, or even stones, trees, animals, and plants?

We know from our own experience of family that closing the gap in relationships is a gradual process and that it is more a matter of love (that respects the sacred identity of another) than of will. We may not share Francis's emotional response and call out "brother" and "sister"—though we may surprise ourselves on occasion—but we can practice seeing the sacred in every person and creature we encounter. We can fight the tendency to see them as separate and unrelated to us.

Francis's own vision of kinship grew strong because he insisted on seeing all aspects of creation—whether people, forests, streams, rivers, buffalo, or field mice—in light of their original relationship with the Creator and only secondarily in relation to himself. He invites us to do the same. We should treat each person and creature with reverence and give thanks for their presence in our lives because they bear the hidden mark of divinity. Using Martin Buber's terms, we should ask ourselves whether our dominant orientation toward people and creatures is governed by an I-It approach that treats others primarily as objects or an I-Thou approach that appreciates the hidden dignity in those we encounter. The "creation story" traces all physical reality, including humanity, to a common origin, a small particle of matter from which a multitude of galaxies, each with billions of stars and planets, have evolved. It outlines an organic model that includes interrelationships and interdependence among all beings, living and nonliving, along with individuality. Approaching this story from a faith perspective, how can we not help imagining our kinship in relation to a shared Source of life in this context? We are intimately related to the universe, having emerged from it.

During a recent television interview a scientist revealed that her reflection on the unlimited possibilities of life in the universe had given her a surprising insight: For the first time, she understood that she was not only a member of an Earth community but of a cosmic community.

Though he worked from a radically different model of the cosmos from ours, Francis heightens our sense of kinship today. In his famous "Canticle of Brother Sun," he reveals a cosmic sense of kinship that had been maturing for a lifetime. He addresses Sun as brother and Moon as sister and invites us into a world that preserves a family relationship between all beings: "All praise be yours, my Lord, through Sister Moon and Stars...."

Practice looking beyond externals and treat those you meet today, people and creatures, with care and tenderness, keeping in mind that each is a creature of God.

Prayer

Let every creature
in heaven, on earth,
in the sea and in the depths,
give praise,
glory, honor, and blessing
to Him…
For He is our power and strength….

—St. Francis

AT HOME IN THE UNIVERSE

True piety…had so filled Francis' heart and penetrated its depths that it seemed to have appropriated the man of God completely into its dominion.

—St. Bonaventure, *The Life of St. Francis*

Perhaps one of the most obvious reasons that Francis touches our hearts today is that he knew how to be at home on the planet and in the universe. He was acutely aware of himself as a pilgrim for whom this world was a temporary dwelling; yet he had a deep awareness of belonging. In our modern culture, we struggle in our relationship with planet Earth, and the universe itself seems vast and impersonal.

In an early allegory about Francis, the "Sacred Exchange," the saint, his brothers, and Lady Poverty enjoy a simple meal and then sleep. When Lady Poverty rises, she asks to see the cloister. Instead of taking her to a building, Francis and his companions lead Lady Poverty to a hill and point to an endless horizon saying, "This, Lady, is our cloister." Francis did not see a world locked in by physical boundaries but one that was primarily Spirit. Paradise itself was not confined to a particular space but unveiled itself underfoot as he walked.

It is easy enough to say that Francis envisioned a world that was God-centered and ultimately gracious and compassionate, but how can we share his outlook today in our secular culture, in a world stripped of sacredness?

In his biography of Francis, St. Bonaventure begins a chapter on the saint's relationship with the natural world with a reference to piety. Piety, he says, filled Francis's being, drawing him to God and to reconciliation with all creation. This translation of piety seems strange to us because the word *piety* has lost its root meaning today. It originates in the Latin *pietas* and refers to love, affection, devotion. It is the attitude shared by family members toward one another. Piety includes the devotion between husband and wife, the love of brothers and sisters for each other, and the affection between children and parents. It also extends to animals, land, buildings, tools, and all that encompassed the life of a household.

Fundamentally, the Latin *pietas* implies a profound sense of being at home, comfortable and at peace because you feel a connection with the world around you. Because Francis dedicated his life to God above all else, his household included all beings under God's roof; in other words, humanity, all creatures, planet Earth, and the universe. His ministry, too, extended to animals, plants, earth, and sky.

If we nurture our relationship with the living God, the Trinity, as Francis did, we will know love and peace at the center of our hearts and at the center of physical reality. We will also find ourselves at home. We will look at people, plants, stars, fields, and animals, and the warmth of love will fill our hearts. Our response will be one of reverence and gratitude. Remembering what it means to be at home ourselves, we remain aware that all beings share the same home.

From the visionary solitude of his hermitage, Thomas Merton admitted that "the universe is my home and I am nothing if not part of it."

Do we feel at home in our immediate family? How far does our sense of home extend? Whom and what does it embrace?

Prayer

All you peoples, clap your hands;
raise a joyful shout to God.
The God of Love chooses us for our inheritance...
Sing praise to God, sing praise,
for God is the Most High over all the earth.

—Psalm 47:1, 2, 4, 6, 7

II
Opening the Heart

Francis repeatedly draws our attention to our hearts....
In a variety of ways, he asks us: Where is your heart?
What is in your heart?
—Regis J. Armstrong, O.F.M. Cap.

Francis's entire life was a journey of a heart that was generously sacrificing for the sake of love. When he wrote in his rule, "Let us love the Lord God with all our heart..." he expressed the hunger for the fullness of God's life in his own life, in the lives of others, and in the world. He challenges us to protect our own hearts so that the Word might grow and flourish.

Of course, responding to God with our entire heart is not easy, and we find many setbacks with our progress. Yet, according to Francis, we are called to let go of any obstacle to this love, hold back nothing to experience the strength and security of God's embrace. By remaining in touch with this dynamic core at the center of our lives, we are able to encounter people and creatures with compassion and feeling, with respect, affection, and gentleness. We are able to appreciate beauty and enjoy the wonders of the universe with the eye of a contemplative.

As we take up this journey of the heart, we learn to give praise and thanks to God in everything we do. Let us now begin this adventure of love that leads into uncharted territory, into the unknown depths of God's own love.

HEART SENSE

Let us love the Lord God with all our heart, all our souls and with all our mind and all our strength...with every effort, every affection, every emotion, every desire and every wish.

—The Earlier Rule

What is the "spiritual heart?" It is our deep longing for God, the center of our humanness. Francis recognized the hunger for the fullness of God's love in his own life, in the lives of others, and in the world. In the early days of his conversion, he walked into the abandoned church of San Damiano and knelt before its Byzantine crucifix. He prayed: "Most High, glorious God, enlighten the darkness of my heart...." From the beginning, Francis had a strong awareness of a center where he struggled to discern God's will.

As adults in a busy world, we find it difficult to act from a heart center. We are too often tired, distracted, or goal oriented. We think too much, and our thoughts are the source of anxieties, guilt, and fears. We allow ourselves to be pulled into the past, into the future, and into fantasy. Thoughts split our minds from our hearts.

Francis reminds us of our fundamental desire for wholeness. We yearn to integrate mind and heart. We begin by first getting in touch with our heart, in other words, cultivating a desire for God's love. In time, thoughts will be guided more and more by a deeper spiritual energy. We will experience the revelation of the Spirit in the here and now—in these people, these birds, this landscape. The heart knows no boundary and gives us the capacity to engage others and the world with surprising intimacy and as truly unique and deserving of our respect.

Francis's childlikeness was a sign that he truly acted from his heart-center. He knew that he could not make himself a child of God—he simply needed to open his heart and allow God to love him. Responding to God's presence like a child who trusted completely in a loving Parent, his relationship with God was spontaneous, uncluttered by ambition and calculation. Rather than promote his own agenda or hide behind fear, anxiousness, and other barriers to trust, Francis humbly accepted the mystery of his life and relied on the guidance of the Spirit.

Cultivating a childlike trust of God in our own lives, we do not forfeit but enhance our deepest selves. Like Francis, we will uncover an unusual sensitivity to people, animals, landscapes, and special places. The world will come alive and possess soul. The Spirit will reveal itself in surprising ways, unleashing a dynamic energy in all our relationships. Truly, a life is measured by the capacity of the heart.

What barriers surround your heart now and keep you from a deeper relationship with yourself, others, and the world?

Prayer

Most High, glorious God, enlighten the darkness of my heart.

—St. Francis

COMPASSION

His soul melted at the sight of the poor and the infirm, and to those to whom he could not extend a helping hand he extended his affection.
—St. Bonaventure, *The Life of St. Francis*

Meister Eckhart tells us that when we touch the heart-center to any degree, we begin to "melt." We overflow into all parts of our lives and infuse them with the reality we found at the deepest dimension of the soul. St. Bonaventure describes Francis as a kind person who "melted" when he saw a poor person or a leper.

Just as Christ identified with "the least of my brethren" (Matt 25:40), Francis practiced compassion, a pouring out of self. The word *compassion*, derived from the Latin *com-passio*, means "to suffer with" and implies a degree of empathy that elicits some kind of response. Francis firmly believed that each person was created in the image of Christ and that to respect a person is to respect Christ in that person.

Spontaneous and open self-giving was at the core of the gospel for Francis. His response to the poor was to help them whenever or wherever he could with no concern for personal cost. He gave them the clothes off his back, altar decorations, food, and if he saw one of them carrying a heavy load, he took it on his own shoulders. In response to a poor man begging for alms, Francis, who had nothing to offer, cut off part of his tunic so that the man would not leave empty handed.

There were times, though, when Francis's compassion was tested. On one occasion, a particularly rude and offensive leper was causing problems for the friars. Francis went to treat the leper and greeted him with a sign of peace. The leper refused the salutation and complained to Francis that not only had he not received peace from God, but also that the friars who were supposed to console and care for him were insufferable.

At this point, Francis offered to wait on the leper and to do "whatever he wished."

"Very well," said the leper. "I want you to wash me from head to foot, for I stink so badly that I am disgusted with myself."

Francis obliged the leper, and as he touched him, the disease disappeared. When the leper saw that he was healed, he wept and begged forgiveness.

Perhaps the greatest lesson that Francis teaches us is that compassion spirals outward in wider and wider circles and includes those who present themselves as unlovable. When it is nurtured and strengthened by the Spirit of Christ, it may be tested—but it will grow, and it knows no limit.

Just as Francis saw the face of Christ in the poor and suffering, he saw the flash of divinity in mountains and seas and developed a caring relationship with animals. He saw himself as a Christlike servant of nature. He empathized with creatures who were suffering or ignored, identified with them, moved inside them. He was not satisfied with distance and insisted on sharing their lives. Like him, they were children who were dependent on a loving Parent, and they needed his care.

Through our own openness to the Spirit, kinship grows; we awaken to the pain and suffering of others and learn the depth of our connectedness and the possibilities for healing. We feel compelled to share brokenness, embrace our roles as cocreators with the Spirit, and cry out with those who suffer, including planet Earth.

Which voices of the Earth community cry out in your own heart?

Prayer

May we love our neighbors as ourselves
by drawing them all with our whole strength to Your
    love
by rejoicing in the good fortune of others as well as our
    own
and by sympathizing with the misfortune of others
and by giving offense to no one.

—St. Francis

THE EYE OF A FOOL

Who would be able to describe the pleasure he enjoyed while contemplating in creatures the wisdom of their Creator, his power and his goodness?
—Thomas of Celano, *First Life of St. Francis*, XXIX

Francis amazed his companions with the sheer delight he took in seeing: They often found him overwhelmed with wonder and awe as he gazed at the sun, the moon, the stars, or a beautiful landscape.

He became emotionally engaged in whatever he saw, reveling in his connectedness with the world. It was obvious that contemplation did not remove him from the world but prompted him to embrace it with unheard-of passion and sensuousness. He did not hesitate to use his senses—smelling, tasting, and caressing. The experience intoxicated him and made him ecstatic. "How great a gladness do you think the beauty of flowers brought to his mind when he saw the shape of their beauty and smelled their sweet scent?" asks Thomas of Celano.

We can identify with Francis's delight and wonder when we slow down and pay attention to the world around us. While working in a garden, walking a forest path, spending time at the beach, we stop and gaze in openhearted wonder. We find ourselves letting go of preoccupations and worries, thoughts of the future or of the past, and we simply let our hearts be filled by the surroundings. We allow ourselves simply to be, and seeing draws us into an intimate relationship with the loving energy that charges the world and heals our spirit. We are not alone in our contemplation but are accompanied by the universe. In the words of Abraham Heschel, we realize that "we do not wonder at things any more; we wonder with all things."

Contemplation as a way of life, however, comes at a price. To see consistently into the heart of things and to enter the mystery of the other, we need to cultivate an inner poverty. We need to let go of our own importance, take a risk, and see the world as a gift.

In his biography of Francis, G. K. Chesterton describes a time when Francis entered a cave and underwent a radical transformation. He entered the cave with one view of the world and left with another; he went in seeing as an ordinary person and came out with the eyes of a fool. Francis's foolish perspective was due to his unique vision of a world completely dependent on God. For most people, the visible was the primary basis for seeing; for Francis, the invisible, the Spirit present within all life, was the fundamental reality. Most are satisfied with finding God in the world; Francis saw the world in God.

When we have eyes to see, says Thomas Merton,

> there is not a flower that opens, not a seed that falls to the ground, and not an ear of wheat that nods at the end of its stalk in the wind that does not preach and proclaim the greatness and the mercy of God to the whole world. There is not an act of kindness or generosity, not an act of sacrifice done, or a word of peace

and gentleness spoken, not a child's prayer uttered, that does not sing hymns to God....

Contemplation not only introduces us to mystery and beauty but also heightens our intolerance for evil and suffering. We find ourselves assuming a prophetic stance. Francis's own gifted perception reinforced his mission to preach the gospel and awaken people to God's loving presence in the midst of ugliness and evil. Today his contemplative vision would increase our sensitivity to the destruction of the natural world and to the dehumanization inherent in the disintegration of cities and our tolerance of slums. It would show us how easily we close ourselves off from the world around us and, no longer feeling a connection, exploit people and natural resources.

Somewhere in his extended poem, *The Centuries*, Thomas Traherne writes that we should learn to see creation through the eyes of God. In the context of Francis's experience, we realize that to see creation through the eyes of God is to see it immersed in a divine light, a light that at the same time we witness within ourselves.

Gaze at something in particular, an herb or a child's hand, for example. See it from the heart and appreciate its mystery and uniqueness. Let its color and form draw you into its center. Feel its texture and smell its scent. Gaze in wonder.

Prayer

You are Three and One, Lord God of gods...
You are beauty, You are meekness...
You are strength; You are refreshment.
—St. Francis

LOVING FRIENDSHIP

...Wherever the brothers are and in whatever place they meet other brothers, they must greet one another wholeheartedly and lovingly, and honor one another without complaining.

—*The Earlier Rule*

There is a mysterious quality about close friends. When their paths first cross, they know in their hearts that the relationship was meant to be and that it transcends words. With each passing year, they celebrate the sheer giftedness of the relationship, knowing that God has brought them into each other's lives for a purpose and will influence others through them.

Francis had a strong sense of friendship with his brothers, a deep empathy and feeling for their needs. He turned to his good friend Brother Leo one day and addressed him tenderly, "May the Lord bless you and keep you; may the Lord bless you, Brother Leo." He preferred some friends to others for companionship; this is the experience of saints as much as it is for us. He also placed each brother before himself and before any spiritual ideal. On one occasion, a brother who was fasting became weak and sick. Francis broke his fast, set the table, and sat down to eat with the brother. He showed him through his example that love was more important than asceticism.

The Franciscan brotherhood was truly a community of gentleness and loving friendship. Francis did not hesitate to employ a feminine model for relationships, treating his companions with motherly love and advising his brothers to be mothers toward one another. His gentle and affectionate way of relating expressed itself in his tendency to call others and everything in nature brother or sister.

Francis fostered deeply loving friendships beyond his fraternity with women such as Jacopa Settesoli, but particularly with Clare, who referred to herself as a "little plant" of Francis. We know that she not only followed the lifestyle of Francis but appropriated it for her own journey and the journey of the women in her community. Francis respected her wisdom and turned to her for guidance. At one point in his ministry, uncertain about his future and wondering whether he should continue to preach or seek out solitude, he solicited Clare's opinion. She advised him to continue his apostolic way of life, and he took her counsel to heart.

Clare's faithfulness to Francis challenged the church hierarchy and the Franciscan brotherhood, especially after the saint's death when she insisted on following Francis's love of poverty to the letter. In ages to come, her strength of character would continue to shape the Franciscan community of both men and women.

Francis celebrated his friendship with Clare in a dramatic meal at the Portiuncula ("the little portion"), which Francis called home for himself and his brothers. The shared meal was Clare's idea so that they could enjoy each other's company. Francis responded to the gift of her presence with a prayer.

Before dinner was even served, he began to speak of God, and all were immediately overcome by the Spirit. They sat in contemplation while people from Assisi saw the chapel and the forest around it go up in flame. Convinced that the fire was real, the townspeople ran to save the structure, only to find the small group sitting around a table immersed in prayer.

In the end, just before his death, Francis returned to San Damiano and the security of his friendship with Clare and her community. It was a dark time because of his suffering, but Clare's love helped renew his spirit and reclaim the abundance of joy that he readily expressed in the "Canticle of Brother Sun." In the canticle, Francis refers to Sister Moon and the stars as "clear and precious and beautiful." Perhaps, as Regis Armstrong suggests, he was referring to Clare, whose name means "clear."

Which friend(s) has become a spiritual guide for you? Take a moment to rest in the light and joy of your friendships.

Prayer

Loving God, may the love between Francis and Clare challenge me to seek greater personal growth in my own relationships, especially with those who have become soul friends.

CREATURES AS COMPANIONS

A nobleman from Siena sent a pheasant to Francis when the saint was sick. Francis eagerly accepted the gift, not with the intention of eating it, but in the way he always rejoiced over such things, out of love for the Creator. And he said to the pheasant: "May our Creator be praised, brother pheasant!" And to the brothers he said: "Let us see now if brother pheasant will stay with us, or if it will go back to its usual and more suitable haunts." One of the brothers took it, at the suggestion of the saint, and placed it at a distance in the vineyard. Immediately, however, it came directly back to Francis' cell....The saint then ordered it to be fed with care, embracing it and caressing it with soft words.

—Thomas of Celano, *Second Life of St. Francis*, CXXIX

Do you remember the pets—dogs, cats, turtles, fish—that were part of your history? Recall the way they influenced your life and the lives of family members, how their everyday presence transformed your environment.

Francis did not hesitate to engage creatures in a friendly interaction. He chatted with them as if they could communicate, and he cherished them as companions in solitude and prayer. Those who lived with him witnessed his deep affection and respect for animals and the pleasure they gave him. Francis identified not only with animals but also with fish, birds, insects, and even plants and rocks. We are told that he was in the habit of picking up worms and placing them at the side of the path so that travelers would not trample them. Certain creatures, such as lambs, captured his heart both because he enjoyed and loved them in themselves and also because they reminded him of the gospel image of Christ.

Creatures recognized that they were loved and respected and often responded in their own unique way. Once he affectionately chided a rabbit for being caught in a trap. The rabbit refused to leave him and eventually had to be released in the woods. On another occasion, when Francis was in solitude at Mount La Verna, a falcon acted as an alarm clock, waking him up for prayer when he overslept because of tiredness.

Francis demonstrated a reverence for creatures because he respected the dignity, unrelated to us, which they received from the Creator. When we treat creatures primarily as "pets," we tend to take them for granted and see them only in the way they fulfill our needs. Advertising, movies, and the media have influenced the way we relate to animals by reducing them to caricatures, tame zoo inhabitants, or entertainment. We forget that a relationship with a creature should be mutual, equal. A blind person, for example, respects and cares for a Seeing Eye dog, and the dog in return offers companionship and guidance. An elderly or bedridden person expresses gratitude for the healing presence of an animal.

Francis shocks many who insist on our dominion over creatures when he writes: "Every creature under heaven serves and acknowledges and obeys its Creator in its own way better than you do." According to Francis, a creature's relationship with its Creator is innocent and immediate, whereas humans have the capability of destroying relationships with their willful disobedience. Creatures spontaneously give praise to the Creator by simply being what they are meant to be; humans offer praise reluctantly or not at all.

How has your relationship with animals influenced your relationship with people?

Prayer

Jesus, teach me humility in my relationship with all creatures. Teach me how to give myself to others, both to human and to natural creatures.

PRACTICING COURTESY

Brother Fire, the Lord created you as something noble and useful among all creatures. Be courteous to me in this hour, for I have loved you and will continue to do so for the love of the Lord who created you.
—The Legend of Perugia

Today the word *courtesy* refers to good manners—holding the door open for an elderly person, letting someone take your place in line. In Francis's time, it referred to the way in which one conducted oneself in court, or the behavior expected of a knight. Francis himself fed his imagination on chivalric tales and dreams of knights who practiced courtesy.

However, as the spiritual leader of a brotherhood, Francis retranslated courtesy. Because all creation was interwoven, a divine family—a family that included even inanimate elements—each part of it deserved love and respect from another. He counseled his friars to be courteous to each other, to the poor, to people of every kind—and to all creation. After all, a courteous Creator gave us life; should we not show the same generosity by treating others, whether people or creatures, with reverence?

In Francis's eyes, we are never isolated but always in relation, therefore always receiving and responding to the gifts we inherit from the world around us. Encounters are charged events. We need to keep our hearts open, receive with an ongoing sense of gratitude, and respond with courtesy. Courtesy, in this sense, is not behavior we feel obligated to perform but a spontaneous gesture of compassion that rises in the depths of the soul when we trust the wellspring of love that graciously flows through us and binds us to all creation.

We can identify with Francis's respect for people and animals, but it is more difficult to understand his ongoing dialogue with primal elements like fire and rain. Toward the end of his life, Francis had an eye infection cauterized with a white-hot iron. Before the iron was applied, Francis asked the fire to be gentle with him. Courtesy is also a two-way street. Francis extended courtesy to Brother Fire but asked that the same courtesy be shown toward him. Such a profound sense of relatedness may surprise us, but it makes sense when we recall how intimately Francis shared the energy of the Source of all life.

Francis's vision of courtesy pervades the "Canticle of Brother Sun." He praises Earth for its courtesy toward us: bringing forth plants, giving us air to breath, water to drink, and so on. In gratitude, should we not reciprocate with an act of courtesy toward Earth? Today, we realize that our lives depend on the oxygen supplied by trees and plants, and we return the courtesy by protecting them from pollutants. A world of mutual courtesy leads to responsible action and reinforces our fundamental relationship with the planet.

We fear passing along to our children a ravaged environment, but an even greater fear should be that our children will inherit from us an attitude toward the natural world devoid of courtesy. In *The Dream of the Earth*, Thomas Berry comments: "If the earth does grow inhospitable toward human presence, it is primarily because we have lost our sense of courtesy toward earth and its inhabitants." For centuries a variety of religions have stressed that all forms of creation are united with us on this planet and that we need to learn to love and respect them. We are beginning to listen.

Courtesy begins when we notice the graciousness of small events: a fire on a cold winter's day; the sound of rain tapping on the roof as we fall asleep. What small event are you thankful for today?

Prayer

My Lord, I am entirely yours....Who indeed has anything that is not Yours? Therefore when we offer You anything, we give You back what is Yours. So what can I offer to You, the Lord God, King of Heaven and earth and all creation? For what do I have that is not Yours?

—*The Little Flowers of St. Francis*

PRAYING WITH
A NIGHTINGALE

Once when Saint Francis was about to eat with Brother Leo he was greatly delighted to hear a nightingale singing. So he suggested to his companion that they would also sing praise to God alternately with the bird. While Leo was pleading that he was no singer, Francis lifted up his voice and, phrase by phrase, sang his duet with the nightingale.
—A *New Fioretti*

Recall a time when you heard the beautiful melodic song of a bird. Did it strike a chord in your soul? Did you find yourself stopping for a moment and appreciating the world around you?

There is a story about a tenor who, while singing, was joined by a mockingbird who stayed with him until the end. When the tenor finished, he turned toward the mockingbird, applauded it, then turned toward the audience and bowed. Francis, too, humbly recognized that he did not sing in isolation but in unison with the creatures around him. The world was alive with praise, and he added his own voice, even responding to the chirp of a cricket. The song he shared heightened his longing for God, a longing he knew he shared with all creation.

We don't usually think of our interaction with creatures as prayer, but when we are awake to the presence of the divine at the heart of daily events, everything in life can become prayer. Think of taking your dog for a walk, stroking a cat on your lap as it cuddles and purrs, chatting with a pet bird. All of these playful moments are prayerful when they engage you fully. When your whole heart is in the moment and you feel that you are connected to a deep inner peace, the peace of God, then you are praying.

Francis had no difficulty accepting creatures as companions in prayer when others might consider them distractions. He believed that God would be just as pleased with the praise of creatures as with his own prayers. Once while Francis was crossing Lake Rieti in a boat, a fisherman offered him a large fish. Francis joyfully accepted the gift and addressed the fish as brother. He then placed it at the side of the boat and began to pray. As he prayed, the fish played near the boat and did not leave until his prayer was finished.

Once there was a monk who heard a bird singing and stopped to listen in a way he had never listened before. When he returned to the monastery, his fellow monks did not recognize him, and he looked at them as if they were strangers. Only in time did he realize that his listening was so complete that time stopped and he had entered eternity. This story hints at the mysterious world that Francis shared with creatures he encountered in the depths of prayer. He entered an enchanted realm where mutual love and respect reign, where a sense of God's earthly presence is available to all, creatures and humanity alike.

Take time to play with an animal, and lose yourself completely in the activity.

Prayer

Sing Yahweh a new song!
Sing to Yahweh, you lands!
—Psalm 96:1

INNER AND OUTER
LANDSCAPES

While resting under an oak tree, St. Francis began to study the location and the scenery. And when he was absorbed in this contemplation, a great number of all kinds of birds came flying down to him with joyful songs, and twittering and fluttering their wings.
—The Little Flowers of St. Francis

It is easy to enjoy a landscape today as casual onlookers, but do we take seriously the notion that the Spirit can draw us to a particular place for revelation? How often do we forget ourselves and bathe our souls in surroundings that speak to us? What landscapes mark the history of our spiritual journey?

From the stories that surround his life, we see that a common way of prayer for Francis was to immerse himself in the sights, sounds, smells, contour, and creatures of a landscape. He valued a sensuous connection with the world. He did not immediately close his eyes and move inward but found the Spirit in the creatures and surroundings. He allowed this rich experience to draw him deeper into God's presence.

Francis's love for the wildness of mountains, rivers, and forests makes one appreciate how much the landscape expressed his soulscape. This is particularly true of Mount La Verna, the mountain retreat where Francis received the stigmata. Though pilgrims flock to the site today, the crowds do not diminish the sense of wildness. The massive rock formations, thick, lush forests, and jagged contours of the landscape still seize the imagination and remind the visitor of the truly radical nature of Francis's spirituality and his single-minded dedication. Francis was drawn here because Christ himself frequented wild landscapes and found shelter in caves. It is easy to imagine that, like Christ, Francis did not so much choose this place but was led to it by the Spirit.

Today we have assumed the role of spectators. We enjoy landscapes from car windows or office cubicles. A world of technological sophistication increasingly removes us from trees, plants, and animals and comforts us with virtual reality. We live in a secular culture that no longer trusts the Spirit's invitation to find God's loving presence in the natural world. We need the help of artists, biologists, saints, and mystics to look at the landscape differently. Describing the peculiar quality of the Arctic wilderness, Barry Lopez alerts us to "something fleeting in the land, a moment when line, color, and movement intensify and something sacred is revealed, leading one to believe that there is another realm of reality corresponding to the physical one but different."

We can also discover the powerful resonance between the outer and the inner by seeking out landscapes that speak to us. A woman went to the shore for her retreat, and as the days passed, she noticed her spirit merging with waves, birds, tossing boats, and sunlight. She discovered that water images in scripture spoke to her in unexpected ways. Appreciating his own love for the Kentucky landscape, Thomas Merton wrote in *The Sign of Jonas:* "For me landscape seems to be important for contemplation; anyway, I have no scruples about loving it."

Follow your own passion for the light and life of a place by seeking out a landscape—garden, forest path, shorescape, backyard—that reinforces your inner light.

Prayer

> Sing psalms to Yahweh with the harp,
> with the sound of music…
> Let the sea and all within it resound,
> the world and all its peoples.
> Let the rivers clap their hands
> and the mountains ring out with joy.…
> —Psalm 98:5, 7, 8

HOLY GROUND

The holy man loved this place [the Portiuncula] above all others; this
place he commanded his brothers to venerate with a special reverence....
                    —Thomas of Celano, *Second Life of St. Francis*, XII

In the stage play and movie *The Trip to Bounti-*
ful, an elderly woman escapes a tense living situation with
her son and daughter-in-law and undertakes a long pilgrimage back to her childhood home in a small rural town. When
her son finally tracks her down and asks her why she both-
ered to return to an abandoned house and a piece of land
that had lain fallow for years, she responds by telling stories
about her childhood love for the history of the place and the
mystery of the land.

Francis too favored certain places throughout his life: Rivo
Torto, where he and his brothers found solitude in the early
years of the community; Greccio, where he recreated the
Christmas event; and San Damiano, where the cross gave his
life direction. But it was the Portiuncula, a small church that
Francis rebuilt during the early years of his conversion, that
became the place where he and his small band answered the
call of the Spirit to preach to others, that he loved the most
and returned to at his death. He emphatically told his brothers:

"See to it, my sons, that you never abandon this place....For this place is truly holy and is the dwelling place of God."

Today, the tiny Portiuncula is housed in an enormous basilica built in Francis's honor. The basilica looms over the small chapel and stands in stark contrast to its size and warmth. Entering this intimate space, it is easy to imagine the power it must have had for Francis. Flickering candlelight dances on rough-hewn wooden walls, creating an atmosphere of stark simplicity and rugged poverty. Though the space is small, it vibrates with energy. Community life sanctified this space and made it a powerful testament to the love of God. Resident friars sometimes prayed all night, restricted their conversation to spiritual concerns, fasted, and used the Portiuncula as a base to help the poor.

We live in a mobile society that has lost a sense of dwelling and cultivating relationships. We wander from place to place without sensitivity to our loss. Yet, on some level, we realize that our spirit suffers. The Portiuncula reminds us of what it means to be at home with ourselves, with others, and with the land.

By learning to love a particular place, we become aware of our interconnectedness with our immediate neighborhood and with a wider community. Loving a place means getting to know the history of the land and the people and paying attention to the creatures that share our environment. It means creating rituals that reinforce the sacredness of the place: times of silence, prayer, sharing with friends, listening to music. Cultivating our own sacred ground heightens our ability to identify with the needs of the land and people on a global scale. To know the effects of pollution near your home, for example, sensitizes you to the effects of pollution in Mexico and other countries. The Portiuncula was not limited space for Francis; because it was rooted in his heart, it linked him to the planet and to the needs of the poor.

What rituals have you created or would you like to create to celebrate the giftedness and sacredness of your own holy ground?

Prayer

I celebrate the sacredness of my home, gracious God, for you have led me here and given my heart a place to grow in love.

AN ADVOCATE
FOR ALL BEINGS

If I could talk to the emperor, I would beg him, for the love of God, to grant my prayer and to publish an edict forbidding anyone from trapping our sisters the larks or from inflicting any harm on them....I would also like, out of respect for the Son of God...that everyone be obliged to give our brothers the oxen and the asses a generous amount of feed. On Christmas day, finally, all the poor ought to be invited by the rich to a lavish meal.

—The Legend of Perugia

Though Francis could not have imagined our environmental concerns, today he reinforces our ethical responsibility as compassionate people. His spiritual vision, which respects the image of the Creator in all beings, stands in opposition to any mistreatment of the poor and to any tendency toward dominance and cruelty in our relationship with creatures and the earth. We are told that he became disturbed "if he saw a poor person reproached or if he heard a curse hurled upon any creature by anyone."

Advocating for creatures, he rescued lambs from slaughter by bartering his cloak for them; he saved a rabbit from a trap and chided it for its lack of attention; he refused a fish that was offered to him and threw it back into the water. At Christmas, he made a point of providing generous amounts of food both for the poor as well as for stable animals and birds.

In the wonderful passage above, Francis imagines himself confronting the rulers of his day and asking for the rights of creatures. This was a dramatic gesture in medieval times because creatures were primarily considered property and food. Humans ruled over the natural order. Yet, Francis counteracted this cultural perspective because he saw all forms of life as gifts from the Creator and therefore possessing their own inherent dignity. He believed that our primary relationship with creatures should not be one of dominance and control but of gratitude, appreciation, and respect.

Can compassion for creatures heighten our sensitivity to the needs of the poor and vice versa? In Francis's inclusive vision, one form of suffering is inextricably linked to the other. At times the connection is clear to us: for example, a Native American reservation near a nuclear dump; poor communities in areas where water is polluted or soil neglected. Recently, an Episcopal priest who wanted to help asthmatic children in a poor section of a large city found that he had to deal with the effects of pollution in the neighborhood as well. Today, more than ever before, we are learning that the suffering of human beings is linked to the suffering of Earth.

If we have empathy only for humanity, we neglect a bond with the natural world; if we concern ourselves only with the natural world, we neglect our relationship to humanity. This lesson can begin at an early age. A teacher received a passionate essay from a young student on the importance of saving the dolphins. During lunch, the same student began a fight with a classmate. The teacher called the student aside and asked him why his sensitivity to dolphins did not include compassion for his classmates? An embarrassed look indicated that the student understood the contradiction.

Our advocacy for those whose dignity is threatened may not be easy, but if we truly accept creation as an ongoing gift, as Francis did, we are responsible for participating in God's creative process of renewing the world.

Pray for the strength to participate in the divine work of healing and the reconciliation of all beings.

Prayer

> Awake! Defend me!
> Side with me, my God.
> Yahweh, you are just, so do justice for me.
> —Psalm 35:23, 24

PRESERVE THE WILDFLOWERS

*He ordered the gardeners to leave the garden borders untilled so that
the green of the grass and the beauty of the wildflowers in their season
could herald the beauty of the Father of all things.*
—Thomas of Celano, *Second Life of St. Francis,* CXXIV

W̶hat kind of garden do you prefer: a for-
mal garden, well kept and planted in neat rows, or a cottage
garden, free and unrestricted? Whichever one you choose,
one thing is certain: A garden means human involvement.

When Francis asked that the gardener preserve the wildflowers and let the grass grow wild, he chose to recognize the
sheer giftedness of creation apart from human interference.
Things in themselves give glory to God without any help from
us. Francis would not deny the importance of human hands.
He too depended on the natural world for food, warmth,
clothing, and so on. He was deeply appreciative for all that he
received, but he also did not want to forget that the natural
world has its own power and voice, given to it by the Creator.

Today it is easy to get in the habit of seeing nature only in
light of our plans because we see ourselves in a position of control more than ever before in history. What have we lost?
Among other things, a sense of the mystery of the natural

world and an awareness that nature itself reveals beauty and possesses integrity. We may argue about the importance of the Costa Rican rain forest for the preservation of all life on the planet, but do we believe the rain forest possesses value in itself and should be preserved simply because it is God's creation?

How do rain forests, wildflowers, trees, and stones have importance apart from us? By simply being what they were created to be in all their individual uniqueness. In *New Seeds of Contemplation*, Thomas Merton explains, "This particular tree will give glory to God by spreading out its roots in the earth and raising its branches into the air and the light in a way that no other tree before or after it ever did or will do."

People in the Middle Ages felt a deep connection to plants, especially wildflowers. This is obvious from the colorful names they used for the wildflowers: Solomon's Seal, St. John's Wort, and Bachelor Button, among others. We could never regain a medieval perspective on nature, nor would we want to, but if we believe, as Francis and medieval people did, that all nature speaks of divine presence, then we can be at peace with witnessing the glory around us and giving thanks.

Take a moment to gaze at wildflowers bathing in the morning or evening light, bursting with color brilliant as a painter's palette. Let the spectacle light up your soul.

Prayer

> Your goodness shines in every being, Source of life; your love flows through the earth and reaches to the skies. Abiding in you, I see light everywhere.

AN INSTRUMENT OF PEACE

The true peacemakers are those who preserve peace of mind and body for love of our Lord Jesus Christ.
—St. Francis of Assisi, *The Admonitions*

Have you ever felt yourself losing respect for others and taking them for granted—whether people, creatures, or the natural world? What was the source of your disrespect? Was it inner turmoil that had been growing for some time? Did you try to regain a sense of peace through sheer will power?

Francis lived at a time, the thirteenth century, when towns often went to battle against each other and people carried swords and knives for protection. Francis, too, participated in these battles and dreamed of knighthood. As he matured, he realized that peace did not simply mean laying down arms but involved a lifelong process of transformation through the gospels. By changing your own heart, you change your relationship with others and with creation.

Francis became an effective and well-known peacemaker who mediated between rich and poor, men and women, people and creatures. On numerous occasions, he brought rival factions together. Even as he lay dying, he diffused an escalating dispute between the bishop and the *podestà* (town council of Assisi). He added a few lines on the virtue of peace and the value of forgiveness to his "Canticle of Brother Sun." When the lines were read, the bishop and the council (both of whom had great respect for Francis) were deeply moved and asked each other for forgiveness.

In the popular Wolf of Gubbio story, Francis established peace between humans and creatures. A wolf had been terrorizing the townspeople, and when Francis arrived, he confronted the wolf with its wrongdoings. At the same time, though, he extended courtesy and compassion to the animal by engaging it in dialogue, treating the wolf not as a stranger but as a brother. Imagine a wild wolf wagging its tail, nuzzling a small, unarmed friar. Fear dissipated, and Francis demonstrated that people can learn something from a relationship with an animal.

Francis teaches us to face the negative aspects of ourselves and claim our capacity for evil. (Even today, we continue to struggle with our inherited fear of wolves!) If we bury the negative in the unconscious, we will eventually project it onto others, whether creatures or people. Uncovering his demons through prayer and self-reflection, Francis discovered how much he depended on God's mercy and love. Trusting this love, more powerful and abundant than any evil, led to inner healing and integration. Francis saw brothers and sisters when others saw only enemies, envisioned harmony when others could only imagine discord, and worked for reconciliation when others had lost hope.

The Great Tree of Peace in the Native American tradition extends to the sky world and casts roots into the four directions, representing the law of cosmic harmony that includes humans and the natural world. In the "Canticle of Brother

Sun," Francis, too, envisions cosmic harmony with sun, moon, water, all the elements and creatures of Earth. Many traditions join Francis's voice, urging us not to tolerate disharmony because it means separation from the very ground of our lives. For Francis, separation from each other and creation meant separation from Christ who is the center of all reality.

What fears prevent me from finding peace with myself and with others?

Prayer

> Lord, make me an instrument of your peace. Where there is hatred, let me sow love. Where there is injury, pardon. Where there is doubt, faith. Where there is despair, hope. Where there is darkness, light. Where there is sadness, joy.
>
> —attributed to St. Francis

COMPANIONS FOR THE
SPIRITUAL JOURNEY

With a feeling of unprecedented devotion, he savored in every crea-
ture—as in so many rivulets—that Goodness which is their fountain
source. And he perceived a heavenly harmony....
                                    —St. Bonaventure, *The Life of Francis*

Usually we think of the spiritual journey as
the return of all human beings to God. Francis, though,
includes both humanity and all creation. Like the people of
Israel who had a deep sense of connection with the land,
Canaan, and felt that it represented not only the fulfillment
of human destiny but the destiny of all creation, Francis
knew the importance of creatures and Earth in the culmination of our spiritual adventure.

We are familiar with the journey of humanity toward fulfillment, but it is difficult for many to imagine that creation
could be included in this journey. This is primarily because
we no longer feel the intimate participation with the world
that past ages have felt. Our souls are not so easily influenced
by creatures and things of this planet, at least not to the
extent that we imagine them to accompany us on our spiritual journey. However, we find ourselves yearning for a

deeper relationship with the world, one that is not based only on science and technology, but one that is relevant to the whole of human existence. We may realize, more than ever before, that the soul itself corresponds to the deepest meaning of the universe. Francis's own contemplative vision reinforces this intuition.

How do we rediscover a wider sense of the spiritual journey? In the spirit of Francis, we begin with a heart alive with Christ. In other words, if the inwardness of our lives is grounded in Christ's love, we will begin to see physical reality as dynamic and holy and as linked to the human spirit.

Francis understood that any relationship with the natural world centers on Christ. Christ's historical presence influenced the very structure of the universe, and it energized both creation and history. Through his birth, death, and resurrection, Christ transformed the universe and directed history toward its culmination. Just as creation flows out of the Trinity through Christ, it returns to the Trinity through him. The spiritual journey of Earth, then, is related to our own journey back to God.

St. Paul describes Christ as the ground of all reality, the beginning and the end of creation.

> He is the image of the invisible God
> the first-born of all creation,
> for in him all things in heaven and on earth
> were created....
> Colossians 1:15—16

The Word holds creation together and in doing so gives it meaning and purpose. The presence of the "Word" in each creature and thing gives all creation a fundamental harmony and interrelationship that unites it toward God's purpose. To understand the meaning of *Word* today, we need to recall the Hebrew term *Dabhar*, which refers not to our present limited understanding of word, but to the creative energy of God that has the power to give birth to all creation.

Colors, sound, and expressions of the natural world all have the potential to reveal the dynamism of the Word at the heart of things. The light that fills the eye, the molecules that make up matter, all overflow with divinity. When we stand in wonder, do we not recognize an invitation to see into the heart of all reality? Francis reinforces the deep faith that the Word is actually present in all nature and is always speaking to us of God's nearness and revelation. The Word, then, actively binds creation and draws it back to God. Earth, cosmos, and all humanity yearn for home.

In what way has the natural world become a spiritual companion for you?

Prayer

> Triune God, strengthen my belief that "Christ is all and in all" (Col 3:11).

III
Learning to Sing

...his song strikes a new note both because of the solidarity it
expresses between the human and cosmic order and because
of the way in which it conveys an experience of the world as
a single harmonious theophany of God.
                                    —Bernard McGinn, *The Flowering of Mysticism*

Through Francis's example, we see that all of our living
can become a joyful song. Perhaps more than anything else, we
think of Francis as a poet with a song in his heart. In spite of faith
crises, setbacks, and poor health, Francis remained a singer. The song
arose from a humble heart that uncovered an earthly paradise in the
midst of everyday experience.

Singing and dancing, shouting and celebrating, Francis gave witness to the Spirit that inspired him. The same Spirit empowers us
to sing the joy that arises from our hearts. Deep, full joy that flows
beneath the transient events of life is the mark of life in the Spirit.
Commenting on Psalm 96, which begins, "Sing a new song to Yahweh," Dorothy Day asserts, "I don't think we can overemphasize
the importance of song."

When Francis sang, he sang in harmony with all creatures
because he was kin of all things. In his canticle to all creatures, he
shows us how to become one with the song that all things and the
universe itself sings to God. Today, our hearts ache for the song that
reconciles us with ourselves and all beings. We yearn to become
one with the music of the heart and the music of the universe.

ran-

cis

poor and

hum·ble

A SONG OF JOY

Let them be careful not to appear outwardly as sad and gloomy hypocrites; but let them show themselves joyful, cheerful and consistently gracious in the Lord.

—The Earlier Rule

Do you feel that your life is weighed down by demands, worries, and fears? Have you lost a sense of enthusiasm and spontaneity?

We sometimes forget the Spirit of Christ alive within us. We lose our compass, and instead of following Jesus' way of life, we become bogged down in our own agendas. Our spirit becomes heavy because we have lost an inner balance and freedom. We yearn for childlike trust and simplicity so that, once again, we can focus on what is most important.

Following Jesus, Francis uncovered the Spirit everywhere, in his own life, in others, and in nature. Leonardo Boff observes, "The Gospel seriousness of Francis is surrounded by lightheartedness and enchantment because it is profoundly imbued with joy, refinement, courtesy, and humor. There is in him an invincible confidence in humanity and in the merciful goodness of God." Francis's brothers knew him as one who celebrated life, rejoiced in the Spirit, and was often found in ecstasy. He danced and sang in the fields, overcome with the love of God. His rapture made him a fool for God, a clown of the universe. He did not and could not restrain his enthusiasm because he loved God with his entire self and saw God everywhere.

Recall a time when you watched a sunset, and as the light melted on the horizon, you felt music rising in your heart. Did you feel joyful and completely rapt in the moment as if you were feeling the rhythmic energy of some deep and mysterious harmony? Francis alerts us to the word that is spoken in our hearts and at the center of creation. He invites us to respond not only with our voices but with our entire lives.

We usually think of joy in relation to good times, but for Francis, joy could pervade even the darkness. In the greatest self-sacrifice or in personal rejection, he found joy because, no matter how difficult the circumstances or people, he knew that his heart, answering to God alone, remained free. He called all his brothers to respond only to the deepest love and to extend themselves in joyful hospitality in all their relationships.

Awakening to our capacity to live joyfully in the Spirit, each day opens our hearts to a song. It is not our song alone but a shared harmony that we cocreate, a music of love that resonates in the lives of others, especially the poor and powerless, and in the entire natural world. As our lives become immersed in this song, we become filled up with a love. Knowing the rhythm of the Spirit in our lives, in the lives of others, and in the world, we rejoice in it and witness heaven on earth.

When have you tasted the joy that Francis hints at? What experiences continue to uncover the song in your heart?

Prayer

> Sing praise to Yahweh all the earth;
> ring out your joy.
> Sing psalms to Yahweh with the harp,
> with the sounds of music.
> Let the rivers clap their hands
> and the mountains ring out their joy.
> —Psalm 98:4, 5, 8

SINGING IN DARKNESS

During his stay in this friary, for fifty days and more, blessed Francis could not bear the light of the sun during the day or the light of the fire at night. He constantly remained in darkness inside the house in his cell. His eyes caused him so much pain that he could neither lie down nor sleep, so to speak, which was very bad for his eyes and his health....
—The Legend of Perugia

Near the end of his life, Francis found himself in a small dark cell connected to Clare's cloister. He suffered from an eye infection and violent headaches. Both daylight and the light of the fire were too strong for him to tolerate. He found it difficult to eat, and mice, scampering through the cell, kept him from resting and praying. His physical suffering was accompanied by emotional and spiritual turmoil: worries about the future of the brotherhood, and questions about his own mission over the years.

Amazingly, at the center of the darkness, Francis uncovered light. A song emerged: the "Canticle of Brother Sun." He was concerned that we do not appreciate the gifts of creation and too often forget the Giver. His song celebrates the radiant sun, the shining stars, the power of the wind, the movement of water, the playfulness of fire, all the fruits of Mother Earth—and praises the Creator. In the last lines, it addresses the need for harmony among people and the encounter with death.

The song represented not only Francis's reconciliation with himself, with others, and with God, but with the entire universe. The rhythm that he discovered was the same as the rhythm at the heart of all physical reality. The same rhythm could be found in the changing of the seasons, in the transition from night to day, and in the movement of the galaxies. Francis lost himself in God's own creative energy; he became the song.

He wanted to share the divine music, so he told his friars to go out and sing in towns and fields. Perhaps those who heard it would see the world differently or feel a song of praise rising in their own hearts. We can only imagine the power of the song when it was originally sung. Hearers certainly witnessed a rhythm born out of a profound belief in the goodness of the world, a belief that Francis had nourished for a lifetime. Today the song continues in the hearts of those who seek reconciliation within themselves, with others, with God, and with creation.

Francis shows us that, if we rely on the deepest faith, a song can arise from the darkness that surrounds personal or cultural struggle. We can have confidence in the light that pervades all reality and in the new life promised by the resurrection. We need to let go of fear and anxiousness and, letting the Spirit breathe through us, to create new possibilities. The cosmos itself constantly proclaims the glory of God. As human beings, we raise our voices and articulate this praise through their lives and actions. We can no longer ignore the rhythmic energy that connects us to the planet. We can no longer refuse to sing and to celebrate Earth and all her inhabitants. If we do, we jeopardize our own physical and spiritual welfare.

Choose a way of singing that expresses the richness of your own experience: create a piece of music, develop a ritual, get involved in ecological concerns, take time to enjoy the shore, the forest, the mountains, the desert.

Prayer

Read Francis's "Canticle of Brother Sun" slowly, meditatively. Let its spirit fill you and help you envision a world of light and hope.

Most High, all-powerful, good Lord,
Yours are the praises, the glory, the honor, and all the
    blessing.
To You alone, Most High, do they belong,
and no man is worthy to mention Your name.
Praised be You, my Lord, with all your creatures,
especially Sir Brother Sun,
Who is the day and through whom You give us light.
And he is beautiful and radiant with great splendor;
and bears a likeness of You, Most High One.
Praised be You, my Lord, through Sister Moon and the
    stars,
in heaven You formed them clear and precious and
    beautiful.
Praised be You, my Lord, through Brother Wind,
and through the air, cloudy and serene, and every kind
    of weather
through which You give sustenance to Your creatures.
Praised be You, my Lord, through Sister Water,
which is very useful and humble and precious and
    chaste.
Praised be You, my Lord, through Brother Fire,
through whom You light the night

and he is beautiful and playful and robust and strong.
Praised be You, my Lord, through our Sister Mother
  Earth,
who sustains and governs us,
and who produces varied fruits with colored flowers
  and herbs.
Praised be You, my Lord, through those who give
  pardon for Your love
and bear infirmity and tribulation.
Blessed are those who endure in peace
for by You, Most High, they shall be crowned.
Praised be You, my Lord, through our Sister Bodily
  Death,
from whom no living man can escape.
Woe to those who die in mortal sin.
Blessed are those whom death will find in Your most
  holy will,
for the second death shall do them no harm.
Praise and bless my Lord and give Him thanks
and serve Him with great humility.

LANGUAGE OF THE SOUL

Praised be You, my Lord, with all your creatures,
especially Sir Brother Sun,
Who is the day and through whom You give us light.
And he is beautiful and radiant with great splendor;
and bears a likeness of You, Most High One.
—The Canticle of Brother Sun

It is easy to assume that the language of the canticle is simple and naïve. However, place the words in the context of Francis's life and vision, and they immediately begin to reveal hidden levels of meaning. The canticle tells the story of a pilgrim who came home to his heart, to the universe, and to God.

Today our first inclination is to read the canticle as if the words had little depth. We have inherited a surface vision of the natural world today and find it difficult to imagine it in relation to our inner lives. For example, we may find the sun and the moon interesting, even intriguing and beautiful, but do we entertain a connection between them and our heart's deepest hunger? In contrast, Francis's vision, which he shared with people of his time, nurtured a direct relationship between the self and the cosmos. The natural world mirrored his inner life.

Our one-dimensional vision hinders our ability to think concretely and empathetically. We tend to see things as objects for practical use and not in terms of a mutual relationship. We look at a tree, for example, primarily as something that we can name and analyze and eventually process for paper goods or building houses—but not as a mystery we encounter. It is much easier to be abstract and analytical. Francis would not tolerate this limited perspective. He walked the hills and valleys of Northern Italy, and his words sprang from his intimate and charged relationship with the landscape and the people. Like Jesus who recognized the power of such natural images as vine and wine and seed for representing the inner life, Francis readily employed natural images to express the story of his heart.

Sun, moon, and wind, then, became features of an inner landscape for Francis, giving him a way of dialoguing with the Spirit within his life and within all creation. They unveiled his inner journey, mirroring his hopes, fears, dark nights of the soul, and love of light. They healed his spirit and urged him toward deeper transformation. The images of the canticle, in other words, mapped out the story of his life. "In this song," writes Eloi Leclerc in *The Song of the Dawn*, "he gave us the depths of his soul and the secret of his new birth."

By following the guidance of the Spirit toward a deepening intimacy with the natural world, Francis's heart became the center where opposites met: heaven and earth, outer and inner. His deceptively simple language became archetypal; it carried a deep resonance linked to the divine energy in our hearts and at the heart of the universe. As a result, the symbols of the canticle not only express Francis's spiritual history, but also the story of humanity and the universe together on a

journey toward fulfillment. It is truly a cosmic tale that resonates in our hearts today!

*Recall an image from the canticle that touches you personally: stars, sun,
water, moon....As you bring this image to mind, does it not feel as if it is
linked to your soul? Does it conjure up sense memories or memories of special
times? Does it give you a sense of wholeness, of being connected to a deeper
sense of self?*

Prayer

God of joy, let the song, music, and poetry of St. Francis
transform my own way of seeing the world.

SUN AND FIRE

Above all creatures endowed with reason he had a particular love for the sun and for fire. He used to say, "At dawn, when the sun rises, all men should praise God, Who created him for our use, and through him gives sight to our eyes by day. And at nightfall every man should praise God for Brother Fire, by whom He gives light to our eyes in the darkness."

—The Mirror of Perfection

Francis and his companions awoke to the light of dawn and praised God, walked through the Umbrian landscape with the heat of the sun on their backs, and sat around campfires at night gazing into the dancing flame. Both sun and fire were radiant, enduring guides for the journey. They were potent everyday realities that Francis favored above other members of the divine family.

As children, we saw the sun as a bright, joyful globe, perhaps illustrated in a storybook. It was ripe with energy and possibility and seemed to pervade all life. As educated adults, we forget the mystery of the sun and rarely look at it with gratitude or a sense of connection. We see it, rather, as a nuclear furnace and little else. Therefore, we must first imagine Francis's intimacy with the elements if we are to begin to appreciate his reference to sun and fire in his canticle.

Because he identified with the Spirit that blew through it, Francis had a deep reverence for fire, enjoyed its ever-changing shape and pervasive light, and protected it even when it became dangerous and threatened him. He was aware that in scripture fire symbolized the presence of God: for example, tongues of fire and burning bush. Francis himself was seen engulfed in light and fire. One day, the brothers, in a dreamlike vision, witnessed the saint transfigured and riding a fiery chariot like Elijah.

The smaller fire pulls our attention to the greater fire of the universe that it reflects. Francis begins his canticle with a reference to Sir Brother Sun who, he acknowledges, bears likeness to the Most High One. Aware of the divine light that filled his entire being, Francis saw the likeness of God in the sun. He wrote the canticle from the perspective of a transcendent light that bathed the deep interior of his soul and revealed creation as it was meant to be seen, as family. The saint believed that "if we walk in the light as he is in the light, we have fellowship" (1 John 1:7). Light images pervade the canticle in the form of the Moon and the stars and of Fire, and each, in turn, is called beautiful.

Our worldview is not the same as his, but if we follow Francis's lead and uncover the light in our own soul, can we not expect to see this light mirrored in the world around us? William Blake gazed at the sun and saw a multitude of heavenly host, singing Holy, Holy, Holy. Today science reintroduces us to the mystery of light. We see the stunning photographs from the Hubble Space Telescope that reveal the birth of stars out of gigantic columns of coal gas and dust. Gaseous towers 6 trillion miles long rise like stalagmites from a cavern floor, each with a tip larger than our solar system. Gazing at such an awesome display of light with the eyes of faith, do we not feel the desire to say with Francis: "Praised be You, my Lord, with all your creatures, especially Sir Brother Sun"?

Sunlight not only fills our vision, but it greets our soul and invites a response. By participating in a dialogue with Brother Sun, an image of the transcendent Source of all life, we discover a fountain of light overflowing everywhere. We taste the dynamism and fullness of light and realize something of the future toward which all creation is drawn. We also know an inexpressible joy whenever we notice the warmth and radiance of sunlight that accompanies us throughout the day, guiding us toward our destiny and the destiny of the cosmos.

Let the image of light be your companion today. Take time to appreciate it both in the world and in the depths of your own soul.

Prayer

Loving God, be my guide. Illuminate my path, teach me to walk in your presence and witness light everywhere and in everything.

LET EARTH TEACH

When he found an abundance of flowers, he preached to them and
invited them to praise the Lord as though they were endowed with reason.
—Thomas of Celano, *First Life of St. Francis,* XXIX

We are beginning to recognize today that
the natural world is both wise companion and teacher for
our spiritual journey. The rain offers us lessons in renewal,
the sun engenders a warm heart, and a field of flowers tells a
tale of beauty. We know the breath of the Spirit in a breeze
and the unfolding of love in a blossom. Francis's own belief in
the goodness of creation led to an intimate dialogue with
sun, rain, stars, and water. He reinforces our desire today to listen and believe that nature does indeed teach.

Like the people of his times, Francis relied on two "books"
as paths to God: the book of revelation and the book of nature.
He found wisdom in Christ and creation. Just as the book of
revelation can be read on many levels, so can the book of
nature. For example, on one level, Francis admired nature's
usefulness; on another, he drew moral lessons from the behavior of creatures like the larks that he took to represent devoted
friars. On still another, he had a contemplative appreciation of
elements like the sun, which he saw as beautiful and valuable
in itself and as a metaphor for the Son of God.

Unlike others of his time who tended to see nature primarily as a stepping stone to a spiritual world, Francis found nature valuable in its own right and respected the dignity in each creature. He did not read nature superficially but enjoyed it and immersed himself in its mystery. He teaches a contemplative vision that is not satisfied with a one-dimensional interpretation of Earth that limits it to use and pleasure but, believing that Christ is at the heart of creation, insists on the depth dimension of the natural world. "Not to look at nature, not to love it to the full, is to refuse to read a document God has specifically composed for us in His love," advises Carlo Carretto.

How do we learn from the natural world? If we truly believe that creation reflects the Word of God, we can take a leap of imagination and realize that it addresses us. Francis's own vision begins with cultivating poverty of spirit that heightens our awareness of the giftedness of all creation, including our own lives. Grateful for this gift, we become sensitive to the bonds we share with the natural world and that we not only address it but it somehow addresses us. Our response? To listen on deeper and deeper levels—to the silence of a forest at night, to the rhythmic motion of water at the shore, to the rhythm of a hummingbird's wings, to the chatter of a small child. Eventually we are restored to a childlike sense of gratitude and awe.

The entire universe can become a spiritual teacher. This is a humbling thought but also an illuminating one. What can it teach? Through its finiteness, it reminds us of our own incompleteness and hunger for fulfillment. At times of deep harmony with creation, we know something of the final unity of all in Christ. Listening deeply, we anticipate a new

Creation fully established at the end of history when all physical reality will be transformed and redeemed in divine love.

Consider the wisdom hidden in the universe: in galaxies, stars, and supernova. Take time to "listen" to any part of nature that calls to you—animals, garden, fields, trees, ocean, stars. What do you hear resonating in your soul?

Prayer

> Ask the animals, and they will teach you;
> the birds of the air, and they will tell you;
> ask the plants of the earth, and they will teach you;
> and the fish of the sea will declare to you.
> Who among all these does not know
> that the hand of the Lord has done this?
> —Job 12:7–9

DISCOVERING HEAVEN
ON EARTH

*We who lived with him saw him find great cause for interior and
exterior and external joy in all creatures; he caressed and contemplated
them with delight, so much so that his spirit seemed to live in heaven
and not on earth.*

—The Legend of Perugia

Francis was said to have recovered a lost harmony. When he preached to the birds, to flowers, and to creatures of every kind, he spoke not only as one who had a
profound sensitivity to creation, but also as a person who
already lived in this world in terms of the next when all things
will be reconciled. He shocked people into an awareness that
God's earthly reign has already begun. His example reminded
them that the Spirit of the risen Christ is truly at work in the
world. Should they not also believe and participate in it?

What are we to make of this testimony? Some might say
that Francis simply imagined a peaceable kingdom, a tame
world where the wolf lies down with the lamb, ignoring the
obvious suffering and cruelty. However, this is difficult to
accept because he traveled the wild landscape of Umbria,
lived off the land, and experienced a world most of us never

witness: a world of robbers, wild animals, thick forests, mountains, and the silence of endless horizons. He certainly encountered the cruelty of nature, suffering and pain, evil and the limitations that pervade all existence; yet, he proclaimed that world was fundamentally good. He looked at reality and saw stars singing and the earth alive with hope. He knew the imperfection of creation but also anticipated the freedom to which all creation is called.

What is such a vision like today? In *The Hungering Dark*, Frederick Buechner describes a time when he, his wife, and his daughter watched six killer whales perform a beautiful dance with such exuberance that it seemed as if all of creation was caught up in "one great, jubilant dance of unimaginable beauty." Tears welled up in his eyes. He comments: "We shed tears because we had caught a glimpse of the Peaceable Kingdom, and it had almost broken our hearts. For a few moments, we had been part of the great dance that goes on at the heart of creation. We shed tears because we were given a glimpse of the way life was created to be and is not."

According to Thomas Merton, "We do not have to go far to catch echoes of that game, and of that dancing. When we are alone on a starlit night; when by chance we see the migrating birds in autumn descending on a grove of junipers to rest and eat; when we see children in a moment when they are really children; when we know love in our own hearts...."

Yet, there is a difficulty, one that Francis knew well. We are imperfect creatures who tend to choose separation over union; we see ourselves as primarily important and creation as secondary. Francis was deeply sensitive to the tendency to sin that keeps us locked out of paradise. He calls all of us to a change of heart if we want to know heaven on earth. We need to turn away from the inclinations and addictions that separate us from the Source of life and cause us to misappropriate the gifts we have received. Through the grace and forgiveness of Jesus Christ, we find communion with the human family and with the cosmos.

One of the challenges for those who take the "Canticle of Brother Sun" to heart is to avoid falling under the weight of separateness and disharmony and trust in the Spirit. The canticle is more than a poetic celebration of creation; it calls us to have faith that peace and simple unity is possible; that we cannot tolerate disregard for the dignity of people or creatures, and that the Spirit can work through us and transform the world. It teaches us to listen not only to the longing of humanity for God, but also to the groaning of creation for the Creator. Our own desire for fulfillment is shared by all creation, and we must work toward hope in the harmony of a new Creation.

Do I rely on my own limited efforts in my search for peace and harmony with myself, others, and creation, or am I open to the work of the Spirit through me?

Prayer

God of life, give me the wisdom to realize that the struggles of the present anticipate a new Creation.

RESPOND WITH PRAISE

Then he spent the few days that remained before his death in praise, teaching his companions whom he loved so much to praise Christ with him....He also invited all creatures to praise God....
—Thomas of Celano, *Second Life of St. Francis,* CLXIII

We usually think of praise as one form of prayer among many others, but for Francis, it is much more primary, something that should flow through all we say and do. "Aroused by all things to the love of God, he rejoiced in all the works of the Lord's hands," St. Bonaventure tells us.

Praise is a response that affirms the fullness of divine presence all around us, our awareness of a new Creation unfolding. When we recognize the playfulness of divine creativity expressing itself in a multitude of forms, what can we do but cry out praise?

Francis reminds us that the world has already been restored in Christ and the time is now; paradise is all around us. Should we not be living the life of the new Creation in which harmony between all God's creatures has been restored? Should we not be shouting out praise in unison with the whole of creation? It is not as if we have to initiate praise of God or wait for the right time or feeling; we simply enter a river of praise that originated before the universe was created and join the ongoing stream of praise.

Suffering, injustice, and evil, even our own personal brokenness, are encompassed by a prayer of praise and lose the power to claim a primary importance in our lives. They are included mysteriously in our wholehearted trust in the goodness of all things. We may still feel the pull of darkness that exists everywhere, but we have the freedom to open the door to heaven in our midst and bear witness to the singing of the universe. This is truly a gift, one that Francis calls forth from his companions, from all creation, and from us.

Francis encourages us to dream heaven here and now, to let go of our myopia and nurture a vision of the infinite present in each event of our daily lives. Interpreting the Lord's Prayer, which asks that heaven be manifest on earth, he writes, "That we may love You with our whole heart...with our whole soul...with our whole mind...and love our neighbor as ourselves." We uncover heaven, then, by loving God with our entire being, and demonstrating that same love for our neighbor. A simple gospel command, certainly, but following it we discover incomparable fulfillment and joy in the present.

Believing in the dream of heaven on earth, we live with confidence that heaven is not only at the end of our journey but also accompanies us all along the way. At some time or another, we have all glimpsed a new Creation. Our response? Praise wells up in us. Praise assures us that we live daily in the radiance of God; it gives us the strength to choose freedom, a deeper sensitivity to our giftedness, and an awareness of our bond with humanity and creation. Our willingness to sing

and dance an alleluia—this is the sign of life in the Spirit!
This is our ongoing prayer as it was for Francis.

Choose a time when you will sing, chant, or dance an alleluia! Praise God with your whole being today!

Prayer

> This is the day which the Lord has made,
> let us exalt and rejoice in it!
> Alleluia, alleluia, alleluia! The King of Israel!
> Let every spirit praise the Lord.
> Praise the Lord for He is good; all you who read this,
>   bless the Lord.
> All you creatures, bless the Lord.
> All you birds of the heavens, praise the Lord.
> All you children, praise the Lord.
>   —St. Francis,
>   "The Exhortation to the Praise of God"

NAKED UPON THE GROUND

He spent the few days that remained before his death in praise, teaching his companions whom he loved so much to praise Christ with him. He also invited all creatures to praise God…"Welcome," he said, "my sister death." Then to the brothers: "When you see that I am brought to my last moments, place me naked upon the ground.
—Thomas of Celano, *Second Life of St. Francis,* CLXIII

Less than a year after he wrote the "Canticle of Brother Sun," Francis was preparing to die. Even as he approached death, he continued to praise God, calling his brothers and all creatures to join him. He not so much sang but allowed himself to be sung. He had found his voice in the Spirit, and it was the Spirit who now freely sang through him.

Though Francis addressed death as "Sister," he was not taking her lightly. He had engaged her in an ongoing dialogue throughout his life. Francis knew death as a constant companion, a reality which he faced daily in himself, in others, and in the natural world. For some, death's presence may be harsh; for Francis she was the entrance to a new life whose riches he had already sensed. It is important to note, says Eloi Leclerc, that Francis sings about death at the same time he sings about Brother Sun. He believes that divine light penetrates even the darkness of the unknown.

At the end, Francis made one final gesture to poverty. He requested that he be taken to his beloved Portiuncula and his body be placed naked on the ground. Following Jesus, who was stripped naked and died on the cross, Francis, at the beginning of his conversion, stripped off his clothes and surrendered his life to God in the courtyard of Assisi. He would now choose nakedness again. He would end his life like a newborn child completely dependent on his Parent.

By dying in the embrace of the earth, Francis not only reaffirmed his love for the earth but also demonstrated that his journey was rooted in the ordinary, concrete reality that he shared with all things. The natural world had been his companion and reminded him daily of his fragility and finiteness, his ongoing earthly pilgrimage. Images of sky, sun, moon, stars, water, animals, and fire had entered the depths of his soul and transformed him. How could he shun the earth now? The final leg of his journey, his entrance into paradise, then, would be in the company of all creation because all creatures of Earth had found a home in his heart.

As Francis's brothers chanted psalms, the saint breathed his last. Larks flew in great loops and sang loudly over the place where Francis lay. His body was carried to Assisi past the convent where Clare and her sisters waited in expectation to share a last loving moment.

What will our deaths be like? They will remain a mystery, but Francis shows us that we should prepare by thinking of ourselves as naked children who trust completely in a loving Parent, the same Parent who gives life to all creation. In imitation of the awesome love of Christ who was stripped and hung on a cross, Francis guides us on a journey that not only embraces humanity but also welcomes all creatures and all parts of creation. He reminds us of the Spirit in our midst and invites us to sing praise in concert with all creation even as we contemplate our own death and dying.

Am I aware of my own nakedness, my creatureliness, my childlike dependency on Someone greater than myself? Hold a handful of earth and contemplate your own death and your resurrection in Christ.

Prayer

> I am not abandoned to death.
> Open the gates of justice to me.
> I will come in and give thanks to you, Yahweh.
> —Psalm 118:18b, 19

AFTERWORD

Be filled with the Spirit,
as you sing psalms and hymns…
And make music to the God in your hearts,
giving thanks to God the Father at all times
and for everything
in the name of Jesus Christ.

—Ephesians 5:18—20

As Francis extended his arms to welcome Sister Death, one of the friars told the saint that he would be remembered and would continue to be a light and a mirror not only for his followers but also for the church at large. The contemporaries of St. Francis were caught up in his vision of a new way of being. He seemed to be a man from another world, a light that showed them the unlimited possibilities of their own humanness and of relationships. If the world could be imagined as one sublime symphony with God as the conductor, then Francis's song became a great wave of harmony that flowed through the minds and hearts of all listeners and rang through creation itself.

We may have thought that the spiritual path was long and difficult, with little room for rejoicing. Francis, however, through the example of his life, shows us that singing is not optional: God expects it. We may want to emphasize sacrifice, but we are called to sing and praise. Scripture and the psalms repeat the same message again and again: "Sing to your God!"

At the end of his life, Francis refused to give in to the darkness and sounded a note of joy. He opened his heart to the Holy Spirit and released the song that he had been singing in one form or another for a lifetime. He truly had become an instrument, working in the power of the Spirit, his strength made perfect in surrender to the will of God. His message? Be a fool for love. In the world, we strive for power, self-fulfillment; in the kingdom, we seek the lowly place and die to ourselves for the sake of overwhelming love.

It is no mystery that hearing the voice of this medieval mystic and poet today, our own beings resonate. Like the followers who accompanied him along dusty paths, we are so moved that we open our hearts; invite the Spirit to heal personal wounds, fears, and anxiousness; and join the birds, the wind, people, and all creatures, Earth and cosmos, in a song of praise. We freely yield ourselves to God as instruments of peace, compassion, and joy.

BIBLIOGRAPHY

Armstrong, Regis J., O.F.M. Cap. *St. Francis of Assisi: Writings for the Gospel Life.* New York: Crossroad, 1994.

Berry, Thomas. *The Dream of the Earth.* San Francisco: Sierra Club Books, 1988.

Boff, Leonardo. *Cry of the Earth, Cry of the Poor.* New York: Orbis, 1997.

Borg, Marcus J. *The God We Never Knew.* San Francisco: Harper and Row, 1998.

Buechner, Frederick. *The Hungering Dark.* San Francisco: Harper and Row, 1969.

De Sola Pinto, Vivian, and Roberts, Warren, eds. *D. H. Lawrence: The Complete Poems.* New York, 1993.

Ellsberg, Robert, ed. *Carlo Carretto: Selected Writings.* New York: Orbis, 1994.

———. *Dorothy Day: Selected Writings.* New York: Orbis, 1993.

French, R. M., trans. *The Way of the Pilgrim.* San Francisco: HarperCollins, 1965.

Heschel, Abraham Joshua. *Man Is Not Alone: A Philosophy of Religion.* New York: Farrar, Straus and Giroux, 1976.

Johnson, Thomas H., ed. *The Complete Poems of Emily Dickinson.* Boston: Little, Brown and Company, 1960.

Leclerc, Eloi. *The Song of the Dawn.* Trans. Paul Schwartz. Chicago: Franciscan Herald Press, 1977.

Lopez, Barry. *Arctic Dreams.* New York: Bantam, 1986.

McGinn, Bernard. *The Flowering of Mysticism,* vol. III of *The Presence of God: The History of Western Christian Mysticism.* New York: Crossroad Herder, 1998.

Merton, Thomas. *The Sign of Jonas.* New York: Doubleday, 1956.

————. *New Seeds of Contemplation.* New York: New Directions, 1961.

————. *The Seven Storey Mountain.* New York: Harcourt, Brace and Jovanovich, 1976.

————. *A Vow of Conversation: Journals 1964–1965.* New York: Farrar, Straus and Giroux, 1988.

Ryan, John K., ed. *The Confessions of St. Augustine.* New York: Doubleday, 1960.

Steindl-Rast, Brother David. *Gratefulness, the Heart of Prayer.* New York: Paulist Press, 1984.

Sources for the Life of Francis of Assisi

Among the books listed below, the *Ominibus* contains the largest collection of primary resources concerning the life of St. Francis. It includes *The Legend of Perugia, The Mirror of Perfection,* and *A New Fioretti.*

Brown, Raphael, trans. *The Little Flowers of St. Francis*. New York: Doubleday, 1958.

Celano, Thomas of. *First Life of St. Francis*. Trans. P. Hermann. In *Omnibus*. Marion A. Habig, ed. Chicago: Franciscan Herald Press, 1983.

———. *Second Life of St. Francis*. Trans. P. Hermann. In *Omnibus*. Marion A. Habig, ed. Chicago: Franciscan Herald Press, 1983.

Cousins, E., trans. *Bonaventure: The Soul's Journey into God; The Tree of Life; The Life of St. Francis*. Classics of Western Spirituality 20. New York: Paulist Press, 1978.

Habig, Marion A., ed. *St. Francis of Assisi: Omnibus of Sources*. Chicago: Franciscan Herald Press, 1983.

The Writings of Francis of Assisi and Clare

Armstrong, Regis J., O.F.M., and Brady, Ignatius C., O.F.M., eds. and trans. *Francis and Clare: The Complete Works*. New York: Paulist Press, 1982.

Rec. 1/14/02 8:75~